Unchanging Truth for Changing Times
(Biblical Doctrines)

Dr. Alvin A. Low

Unchanging Truth for Changing Times (Biblical Doctrines)
©Dr. Alvin Low. All rights reserved.
www.actsinternational.net, AlvinLow98@yahoo.com

Published by
Lulu Press
860 Aviation Parkway, Suite 300
Morrisville, NC 27560

Printed in U.S.A., 2007.

No part of this publication may be reproduced, stored or transmitted by any means—electronic, mechanical, photographic (photocopy), recording or otherwise—without written permission from the copyright owner.

Scripture quotations, unless otherwise marked are taken from the "NIV" -- *Holy Bible, New International Version* ®, Copyright © 1973, 1978, 1984 by International Bible Society. Used by permission of Zondervan Publishing House. All rights reserved.

Scripture quotations marked "NASB" are taken from the *New American Standard Bible* ®, Copyright © 1960, 1962, 1963, 1968, 1971, 1972, 1973, 1975, 1977, 1995 by The Lockman Foundation. Used by permission. All rights reserved.

ISBN: 978-1-4303-1023-5

Table of Contents

Introduction   Page   5

1. The Doctrine of God (Theology)   9
2. The Doctrine of Christ (Christology)   39
3. The Doctrine of the Holy Spirit (Pneumatology)   75
4. The Doctrine of the Bible (Bibliology)   93
5. The Doctrine of the Trinity   119
6. The Doctrine of Angels (Angelology)   125
7. The Doctrine of the Human Race (Anthropology) 143
8. The Doctrine of Salvation (Soteriology)   163
9. The Doctrine of the Church (Ecclesiology)   189
10. The Doctrine of the Last Things (Eschatology)   207

Conclusion   221

Appendix: The 70 Weeks of Daniel 9:24-27   223

                    Chronological Chart of the End Times   230

Bibliography   231

Introduction

You are about to begin a journey on learning the unchanging truth for changing times. The unchanging truth is the Word of God. It will challenge our thinking, correct our faulty beliefs, clarify our convictions, touch our hearts, bend our wills, and transform our lives.

Paul exhorts Titus: *"You must teach what is in accord with sound doctrine."* (Titus 2:1) Basically, doctrines means teaching. Doctrines are teachings drawn from a literal interpretation of the Bible. A study of doctrines will prevent heresies. 2 Timothy 4:3 warns, *"For the time will come when men will not put up with sound doctrine."*

More than learning about doctrines, I hope our lives will be transformed. We want to move ...

From	*To*
Knowing	Being
Doctrines	Doing
Beliefs	Behavior
Principles	Practices
Creed	Conduct
Orthodoxy	Ortho-praxy
Learning	Living

One of the dangers of studying "doctrines," as is often accused by non-believers and believers alike, is to remain in an ivory tower -- learning the fine points of doctrines without living the doctrines. We must *learn*, and more importantly, we must *live* the doctrines. We must *define* what we believe, but more importantly, we must *demonstrate* what we believe. In many parts of the world, religion is not so much to be studied but to be lived. It is not a compartment of life, but the whole life. Gandhi said that, "It is a first class human tragedy that the people of the earth who claim to believe in the message of Jesus, whom they describe as the Prince of Peace, show little of that in actual life." What an indictment on the church! "When theology is reduced to a mere 'intellectual process' detached from the social and cultural issues, it settles within the domain of the 'unreal.' Exegesis and the concomitant biblical theology can be easily convoluted with some abstract symbols and meanings to denote 'out of this world' concepts and ideas,"[1] unrelated to the struggles of humanity. We will seek to avoid doctrinal irrelevancy as we consider the various doctrines set forth in the Scripture.

Sunil H. Stephens says,

> Doing theology is more like Jacob's wrestling with God, self, and, the world. As Martin Luther said that it is not reading, speculating or understanding that makes one a theologian but living, dying and being damned. Theology is born out of a struggle or tension between the text of the word and the context in which we find ourselves. The context raises issues, questions and may even shed light on the biblical text. The Bible on the other hand, not only gives answers, but also often reformulates the very questions asked....The answers

---

[1] Santos Yao, "The Table Fellowship of Jesus with the Marginalized: A Radical Inclusiveness," *Journal of Asian Mission* (3/1. 2001): 35-36.

that the Bible gives, "…must then be applied to the bleeding sores of a suffering continent."[2]

A brief word before we begin.

1. Keep in mind that the nature of the doctrine may be *exclusive*, but the spirit of the doctrine must be *inclusive*. We may have a set of doctrines which define who we are, but we must not allow the exclusiveness of our doctrines to interfere with our fellowship with one another and our working together with those who differ from us—especially in the fine points of interpretation. For example, Jesus is perfect and sinless, but He never allowed His exclusive sinless nature to prevent Him from reaching and touching sinful humanity. The nature of our message may be exclusive, but the disposition of the messenger need not be exclusive. **In essentials: unity; in non-essentials: flexibility; and in all things: charity.**

2. Speak the truth in love (Eph. 4:15). The articulation of our beliefs does not need to be done in a confrontational manner. Watch out for our *manner* as we communicate our *message*. I am not saying we should be timid messengers. *Boldness* does not mean *bluntness*. Neither does it mean we should not oppose false doctrines. We should by all means oppose false teachings, but let us do so in a loving manner.

3. Traditions may be inconsistent with doctrines. But, wait. Don't begin a revolution in your church. Some long-time traditions are difficult to change. Respect them. Change will come slowly, and some changes are not

---

[2] Sunil H. Stephens, "Doing Theology in a Hindu Context," *Journal of Asian Mission* (1/2, 1999):198-99.

worth the trouble. No church or denomination is perfect. Again, your zeal and knowledge must be tampered with love.

4. There are differences between Christianity and other religions which will be noted in this book. In noting these differences, it will be understood that they are not ammunition for shooting down the non-believer. They are food for the sustenance of the soul, the enlightenment of the mind, and the strengthening our own faith to better communicate the Gospel lovingly to the non-believer.[3] We do not need to attack the non-believer where he/she is weak, rather we should help him/her see his/her weakness. We are not to win a victory by argument at the level of the rational. This is never effective anyway because it is limited to the conscious part of the mind, and its effect may be to deepen the unconscious resistance. We are to make effective contact, and so witness to Christ through love and understanding, and that Christ may make His own entrance into the mind and heart of the non-believer. [4]

5. Be careful in your choice of words to communicate biblical doctrines in your culture. Certain words in a particular culture have completely different meanings from another because of historical and cultural backgrounds. What we say is important. "How" we say "what" we say is also important. There must be a careful choice of contemporary words without changing the Truths.

Enjoy the class, learn the doctrines, love one another and experience the love of Jesus Christ!

---

[3] Frank Whaling, *An Approach to Dialogue with Hinduism* (Lucknow, India: Lucknow Publishing House, 2000), p. 52.
[4] Ibid., p. 70.

The Doctrine of God (Theology)

Objective

To know, worship, and serve God alone.

The Existence of God

1. The Bible *assumes* the existence of God. The Old Testament begins with, *"In the beginning God..."* (Genesis 1:1), and the Gospel of John begins with, *"In the beginning was the Word, and the Word was with God, and the Word was God."* (John 1:1)

2. The Bible *argues* for the existence of God. It argues that from creation there is a Creator God. In Isaiah 40:26, *"Lift your eyes and look to the heavens: Who created all these? He who brings out the starry host one by one, and calls them each by name. Because of his great power and mighty strength, not*

one of them is missing." Similarly the Psalmist says, *"The heavens declare the glory of God; the skies proclaim the work of his hands."* Again in Isaiah 40:12, *"God measured the waters in the hollow of His hand, or with the breadth of his hand marked off the heavens. He has held the dust of the earth in a basket, and weighed the mountains on the scales and the hills in a balance."* Paul argues that there is a *"...living God, who made heaven and earth and sea and everything in them."* (Acts 14:15) Creation testifies to a Creator.

3. God's existence is eternal. There was not a time when He did not exist. He is the beginning and the end. He is the Alpha and the Omega. (Rev. 1:8; 21:6; 22:13)

Modern man and woman have tried to do away with the existence of God. German philosopher Friedrich Nietzsche said that "God is dead" in 1885. The Bible is clear that there is God. God is not dead. He is very much alive.

Stephen W. Hawking denied the existence of God when he wrote that "if the universe is really completely self-contained, having no boundary or edge, it would have neither beginning nor end: It would simply be. What place, then, for a creator?"[5]

Those who denied the existence of God do not want to be held accountable to Him. Unfortunately, they are desperately wrong, no matter how sincere they are. Sincerity does not prove truth. A person can be sincerely wrong. Truth cannot be done away by human suppression (Rom. 1:18). Ultimately, humankind will stand before Him to answer before Him (Rev. 20:13).

---

[5] Stephen Hawking, *A Brief History of Time: From the Big Bang to Black Holes* (Toronto: Bantam, 1988), p. 140-41.

The Revelation of God

1. The revelation of God in nature. Nature reveals the invisible qualities of God—His eternal power and His divine nature (Romans 1:19-20). The heavens are the works of His fingers (Psalm 8:3-4).

2. The revelation of God in human conscience. God has given human being a conscience (Romans 2:14-16) to know right from wrong. But the Fall had darkened human conscience. The conscience can be suppressed to purposely pursue a course contrary to it.

3. The revelation of God in humanity's search for eternity. God sets eternity in human hearts (Ecc. 3:11). Man and woman's search for eternity is a testimony to the fact that He has revealed Himself to the inner beings of His creatures. Humans are wired for God.

4. The revelation of God in Jesus Christ. Jesus revealed God (John 1:18). He is the *"image of the invisible God"* (Col. 1:15). *"In Christ all the fullness of the Deity lives in bodily form."* (Col. 2:9) Jesus said, *"Anyone who has seen me has seen the Father."* (John 14:9)

5. The revelation of God in Scripture. Scripture reveals God. Jesus asserted that Scripture revealed Him (Luke 24:27, 44-45; John 5:39).

6. The revelation of God through specific means[6]:

---

[6] While God can use these various means to reveal Himself to people today, they do not contradict, or supersede the Bible. We must be careful to evaluate such claims against the Bible (1 John 4:1-6). Neither are we to seek after these various means because the Bible is sufficient to reveal Himself to us. We believe in the sufficiency and the authority of Scripture, and yet

a. **Theophanies** – Sometimes God revealed Himself through His appearance, either directly or through the Angel of the Lord. He appeared to Abraham (Gen. 17:1, 22; 18:1), Isaac (Gen. 26:2), Jacob (Gen. 32:30), Moses (Ex. 3:2-6; 33:11), and Gideon (Judges 6:12-18).

b. **Direct Contact** – Sometimes God revealed Himself through direct contact. God revealed Himself to Jacob (Gen. 35:7), Moses (Num. 11:25), Samuel (1 Sam. 3:21, 9:15), David (2 Sam. 7:27, 1 Chron. 17:25), Elisha (2 Kings 8:10), and Jeremiah (Jer. 38:21).

c. **Visions and Dreams** – Sometimes God revealed Himself through visions and dreams to Pharoah (Gen. 41:25), Jacob (Gen. 28:12-16), Solomon (1 Kings 3:5-15), Daniel (Dan. 2:19, 30), and Joseph (Matt. 1:20; 2:13). *"When a prophet of the LORD is among you, I reveal myself to him in visions, I speak to him in dreams."* (Num. 12:6)

d. **Voice** – Sometimes God revealed Himself through a voice from heaven (Gen. 22:1, 11). At the baptism of Jesus, a voice from heaven said, *"This is my Son, whom I love; with him I am well pleased."* (Matt. 3:17) When Paul was on the road of Damascus, he heard a voice saying to him, *"Saul, Saul, why do you persecute me?"* (Acts 9:4)

e. **Miracles and Signs** – God revealed Himself through miracles and signs. For example, He

---

remain open to His various methods if He chooses to do so, but we do believe He will not contradict, delete, or add to His Word.

revealed Himself through the flood (Gen. 6-9), the destruction of Sodom (Gen. 19), the Egyptian plagues, the pillar of cloud and fire, the parting of the Red Sea (Exodus 3-15), the parting of the River Jordon (Joshua 3-4), the sun standing still (Joshua 10), and the miracles of Jesus (John 2:11, 10:38).

    f. **Prophets** – God revealed Himself to His people through the prophets. Amos declared, *"Surely the Sovereign LORD does nothing without revealing his plan to his servants the prophets."* (Amos 3:7) Peter said, *"Men spoke from God as they were carried along by the Holy Spirit."* (2 Peter 1:21)

The Nature of God

    1. **God is a person.** He is not an impersonal force or a principle.[7] He is a person. He has personal Names: He

---

[7] There are several differences between the Christian and Hindu concept of God: (1) In Christianity, God is a person, not an impersonal force. Hinduism considers *Brahman* as an impersonal monistic ("all is one") force, an impersonal oneness. (2) God has attributes, but according to Hinduism, the highest form of *Brahman* is called *nirguna*, which means "without attributes or qualities." (3) In Christianity, the concept of a personal God is never developed over time. God made Himself known as a *personal* God from the very beginning in the Book of Genesis. The Hindu concept of God developed after the *Upanishads* were written -- *Nirguna Brahman* became *saguna Brahman,* which is *Brahman* "with attributes." This personified form of *Brahman* is also called *Ishvara.* According to Hindu tradition, *Ishvara* became known to humanity through the *Trimurti* (literally, 'three manifestations') of *Brahman.* Those manifestations include *Brahma* (the Creator), *Vishnu* (the Preserver), and *Siva* (the Destroyer). *Ishvara* became personified even further through the ten mythical incarnations of *Vishnu,* called *avatars.* The forms of these incarnations include that of animals (for example, a fish, tortoise, and boar) and of persons (for example, Rama, Krishna, Buddha). Epics such as the *Ramayana* and the *Mahabharata,* which includes the popular *Bhagavad-Gita,* tell the stories of these myths. Beyond

is Elohim (אֱלֹהִים Gen. 1:1), Yahweh or Jehovah[8] (יְהוָה: Gen. 2:4), "I Am who I Am" (Ex. 3:14), the Lord (Isa. 45:5), Yahweh Jireh (Gen. 22:14), Yahweh Roi (The Lord... my shepherd, Psa. 23:1), El Olam (The everlasting God, Gen. 21:33), El Shaddai (The Almighty God, Gen. 17:1), Yahweh Nissi (The Lord is my Banner, Ex. 17:15), Yahweh Shalom (The Lord is peace, Judg. 6:24), Yahweh Sabbaoth (The Lord of hosts, 1 Sam. 1:3), Yahweh Tsidkenu (The Lord our Righteousness, Jer. 23:6), Yahweh Shammah (The Lord is there, Eze. 48:35), Qadosh Israel (The Holy One of Israel, Isa. 1:4).

As a person, He wills (Gen. 2:18, 3:15, 16; Psa. 115:3), He speaks (Gen. 1:3), He calls (Gen. 1:5, 8), He sees (Gen. 11:5), He creates (Gen. 1:31), He hears (Psa. 94:9), He loves (2 Chron. 2:11; Psa. 11:7, 33:5), He grieves (Gen. 6:6-7; 1 Sam. 11:15), He repents (Gen. 6:6), He rules (Psa. 22:28, 59:13, 75:7), He disciplines (Deut. 4:36; Job 5:17), He sustains (Matt. 6:26-30), and He judges (Psa. 9:19; Eze. 20:36; Rev. 18:20).

God receives worship (Gen. 8:20, 12:7-8) and praise (Gen. 24:27, Ex. 15:2; Matt. 5:16; Luke 17:18); He hears prayers (Ex. 8:8; Jer. 29:7; Acts 8:22).

2. **God is spirit** (John 4:24). He is immaterial and incorporeal (having no bodily form). Sometimes the biblical authors used human terms such as hands (Ex. 24:11), feet (Psa. 18:9) and eyes (2 Kings 19:16) to describe God. These are anthropomorphic expressions

---

the principal deities of the *Trimurti* and the *avatars,* it is estimated that there are 330 million other gods in Hinduism.

[8] Jehovah is an artificial English word for YHWH and its vowels (YaHoWaH). Adonai is used by the Jews as a substitute for Yahweh because they were afraid to pronounce the name YHWH.

for God. These figures of speech do not mean God has human hands, feet or eyes.

3. **God is invisible.** John 1:18 says, *"No one has ever seen God."* He is invisible (Col. 1:15; Rom. 1:20; 1 Tim. 1:17; Heb. 11:27). When the Scriptures say that men saw God (Gen. 32:30; Ex. 3:6; Num. 12:6-8; Deut. 34:10; Isa. 6:1), it refers to the reflections of God or manifestations of God in visible form such as the angel of the Lord, called Theophanies (Gen. 16:7-14, 18:13-33, 22:11-18, 32:30; Ex. 3:2-5; Judg. 6:11-23; 1 Kings 19:5-7; 2 Kings 19:35). No one can see God and live (Ex. 33:20).

4. **God is alive.** He is the living God (Deut. 5:26; Josh. 3:10; 1 Sam. 17:26, 36; 2 Kings 19:4, 16; Rom. 9:26; 2 Cor. 6:16).

5. **God is indivisible and undividable.** The Lord is one (Deut. 6:4; Zech. 14:9; Mark 12:29; James 2:19). There is only one God (1 Cor. 8:4-6, 1 Tim. 2:5).

The Attributes of God

1. **God is omniscient.** God's omniscience means He possesses (without prior discovery of fact) complete and universal knowledge of all (actual and possible) things past, present and future (Psa. 139, 103:14, 69:5; Matt. 1029, 30; Acts 15:18; Heb. 4:13). The vast sequence of human and physical histories appear all at once, and without any consciousness of succession, to the omniscient God. The latter phrase, "without any consciousness of succession" does not mean God does not know the order of events. What it means is "God knows the things that shall be wrought, and the order of them in their being brought upon the stage of the world; yet both the things and the order, He knows by one act of knowledge... Man knows a succession successively; God knows a succession instantaneously, and

simultaneously."[9] Such knowledge, as the Psalmist declared, is too wonderful, too high for men to attain (Psa. 139:6). Therefore, there is nothing that has happened or will happen that has taken or will take Him by surprise.

While it is true that an increase in human knowledge, as in the world today, does not necessarily lead to wise and careful use of that knowledge, this is not true for God. God is perfectly wise. Being perfectly wise, He ensures the full, perfect and use of His knowledge for His children and the world. Our limited human frame of reference may not enable us to see the good that will come out of a particular tragedy; but God, being wise and omniscient, chooses the right method (though we are prone to question them), and the right reasons (though we may not know them) to achieve the right ends (though we may disagree with them) for His glory and for the benefit of His children.

The fact that God knows all things does present some key theological problems, as often suggested by Christians. Two of the most common questions are: If God knew Adam would sin, why then did He create him? If God knows the outcome of the event, why does Scripture say He repents?

The second question is easier to answer. The word "repent" is used of God anthropomorphically. That is, the biblical authors used a common human figure of speech to describe the action of God. What is seen as "repenting" to the world is already history in the mind of God.

---

[9] William G. T. Shedd, *Dogmatic Theology* (Grand Rapids, MI: Zondervan Publishing House, n.d. 3 vols.), 1:345.

The first question concerns the creation of Adam. Adam was created with a freedom to choose good or evil. Such choices open the possibility for good and evil. God knew in advance Adam would sin, but at the same time He had planned for mankind's redemption. Scripture says Christ was slain even before the foundation of the world. His knowledge of the fall of Adam included His knowledge of the provision for salvation. The fall of Adam provided the opportunity for God to demonstrate His grace in working out His plan of redemption.

There are perhaps many other questions we may not able to provide adequate answers. C.S. Lewis acknowledged this difficulty: "When I lay these questions before God I get no answer, but rather a special sort of 'no answer.' It is not the locked door. It is more like a silent, certainly not uncompassionate, gaze. As though He shook His head out in the refusal but waiving the question. Like, 'Peace, Child; you don't understand.'"[10]

As finite beings bowed in humble submission to the infinite God, we must acknowledge our limited knowledge in comparison to His omniscience. Let not the questions so trouble us that we fail to worship and love Him. We rest in the comfort that He knows all things.

According to the Psalmist, God's omniscience can be both a comfort and a distress in a person's life. The Psalmist speaks of comfort because God knows all things (Psalm 139:1-5):

---

[10] C. S. Lewis, *A Grief Observed* (New York, NY: HarperCollins Publishers, 1961), pp. 54-55.

O Lord, you have searched me and you know me.
You know when I sit and when I rise; you perceive my thoughts from afar.
You discern my going out and my lying down;
  you are familiar with all my ways.
Before a word is on my tongue you know it completely, O LORD.
You hem me in-- behind and before; you have laid your hand upon me.

On the other hand, there is nothing we do or think that will escape God's knowledge. The Psalmist declares that he cannot hide himself from the Lord because He is there (Psa. 139:7-12). Such knowledge is distressful when a believer willfully sins against God.

2. **God is omnipotent.** God is all-powerful and able to do whatever He desires in harmony with His attributes and purpose. Job 42:2 declares, *"I know that you can do all things; no plan of yours can be thwarted."* With God all things are possible (Matt. 19:26), and nothing is too difficult for Him (Jer. 32:17). Indeed, He is the Almighty (Gen. 17:1; Rev. 4:8).

   God is all powerful, but whatever He does must be in harmony with His perfection. God will not do things contrary to His attributes. For example, He cannot lie (Titus 1:2), or be tempted by evil (James 1:13), or deny Himself (2 Tim. 2:13).

   The exercise of His power must be in accordance with His Word. If He contradicted His Word in the exercise of His power, the logical consequence is that His Word could not be trusted. "Why doesn't God remove all sin and evil now?" He chooses not to remove sin and evil *now* because it would contradict His Word. The removal of sin awaits a future time (Dan. 9:24). Because all God does is in harmony with His Word, His Word can be trusted fully and His promises are reliable.

God will not exercise His power contrary to His purpose. For example, He "can" remove the "cup" (Luke 22:42), but it was not His will to do so. His "can-ness" operates within His "will-ness." We are, therefore, to submit to His will while we believe in His power. Daniel's three friends believed in God's power to rescue them, but they also submitted themselves to the will of God. They said to Nebuchadnezzar, *"O Nebuchadnezzar, we do not need to defend ourselves before you in this matter. If we are thrown into the blazing furnace, the God we serve is able to save us from it, and he will rescue us from your hand, O king. But even if he does not, we want you to know, O king, that we will not serve your gods or worship the image of gold you have set up."* (Dan. 3:16-18)

The leper knew this doctrine when he begged Jesus, *"If you are willing, you can make me clean."* (Mark 1:40) The leper believed Jesus "can" make him clean, but he submitted himself to His will. Similarly, Jesus prayed, *"Not my will, but yours be done."* (Luke 22:42)

The possession of all power does not, therefore, mean the indiscriminate exercise of that power. Nor does it mean we can force God to exercise His power. He "can" perform miracles, but He "may not" want to for reasons only known to Him. He has the prerogative to exercise His power without being dictated by us. His omnipotence includes the power of self-limitation.

> God is able to deliver
> From my weariness and pain,
> And He will deliver swiftly
> If it be for lasting gain;
> > But if not – my heart shall sing,
> > Trusting wholly in my King
>
> God is able to supply me
> With abundance from His store,
> And He will supply my table
> Though the wolf be at the door;
> > But if not – my heart shall rest
> > In the thought, "He knoweth best."
>
> God is able to defend me
> From my foes who throng around,
> And He will defend me surely
> When their rage and hate abound;
> > But if not – I'll bless His name,
> > And confess Him just the same.
>
> God is able to save dear ones
> From the world and self and sin,
> And He will both save and keep them
> In His fold safe, gathered in;
> > But if not – He'll hold my hand,
> > Teaching me to understand.

The exercise of His power may be immediate (without the use of intermediary). For example, He created the universe without the use of any intermediary. Then again, He may use an intermediary to exercise His power. For example, He can heal directly without the doctor or medicine, but He may also heal through the use of medicine or a doctor. To demand God exercise His power without the use of an intermediary is to dictate how He is to work. Again, God is not our servant, but our Master.

3. **God is omnipresent.** The omnipresence of God is that perfection of Divine Being by which He transcends all spatial limitations, and fills every point of the universe with His Being without diffusion or expansion, multiplication or division, from eternity to eternity (Psa. 139:7-8; 1 Kings 8:27; Isa. 66:1; Jer. 23:23, 24; Acts 17:27, 28).[11]

Certain truths arise out of this definition. First, God is above and beyond His creation, and He is not subject to its limitations. This aspect is commonly called the transcendence of God.[12] Second, there is not limitation of space to the Divine Being. God is not "diffused through space, so that one part of His Being is present in one place, and another part in some other place."[13] He is wholly present in every place. The omnipresence of God is not by expansion, multiplication, or division of essence. He is all in every place. Third, His omnipresence is from eternity to eternity. There is not a time when God does not fill every part of the universe with His whole Being. Further, the totality of His essence is present at the same moment in all. Fourth, in order for His whole Being not to be bound by space and yet fill every space, He has to be an infinite, incorporeal Spirit present at every point of space as a totality.

---

[11] Augustus Hopkins Strong, *Systematic Theology* (Philadelphia, PA: The Judson Press, 1907. 3 vols), 1:279. Louis Berkhof, "Attributes of God," *The Living God*, ed. Millard J. Erickson (Grand Rapids, MI: Baker, 1973), p. 343.

[12] The doctrine of the transcendence of God therefore rejects pantheism (God in all) and animism (everything is a god).

[13] Berkhof, p. 343.

The omnipresence of God means God is everywhere. He is not bound by time and space. But it does not mean that God is "in" every part of His creation, and that nature is part of God and, hence, to be worshipped. That would be pantheism. God is everywhere, but not "in" everything. The omnipresence of God does not mean He is dispersed throughout the infinite reaches of space, so that every part of space has at least a little part of God. God is present in the room, but it does not mean that God is "in" the chair or "in" the table. Creation is separate from God, but not independent of Him.

God is present in the universe in "His whole Being." The Deists believe God is present in creation with His power, not His being, and God is acting upon the world from a distance. This concept is not consistent with His divine perfections.

While God is omnipresent, He may manifest His *special* presence in certain places. For example, there was a special presence of God in the temple. Sometimes believers sensed a special presence of God at a certain time.

We worship an Almighty God who is omnipresent. He is, therefore, not localized into a small corner of the universe, and we must refuse to localize Him into a tribal god. He fills the universe with His Being. Solomon said heaven and the highest heavens could not contain Him (1 Kings 8:27). God is all-present. In Proverbs 15:3, *"The eyes of the LORD are everywhere..."* Because God is omnipresent, we cannot hide from Him. *"Can anyone hide in secret places so that I cannot see him?" declares the LORD. "Do not I fill heaven and earth?" declares the LORD."* (Jer. 23:24)

4. **God is infinite and eternal.** God has no beginning or end. He is not limited by infinitude. Psalm 90:2 declares God is "from everlasting to everlasting" (cf. Hab. 1:12). He is the "eternal God" (Gen. 21:33). He lives forever (Isa. 57:15). He is immortal (1 Tim. 6:16). His years will not end (Psa. 102:27). He is free from all succession of time, though He knows the succession of events. He viewed the past and the future as one present *now*. He created "time" for His creation, but He Himself is timeless.

5. **God is immutable.** God is unchangeable in His essence, attributes, consciousness and will. He cannot become more wise today than He was yesterday because He is perfectly wise through all eternity. Neither can He be less than He is today. He remains the same (Psa. 102:27, Heb. 1:12). He does not change (Mal. 3:6).

He is immutable in His plan. Scripture says His plans stand firm forever (Psa. 33:11), and He will accomplish His plan (Isa. 46:11). However, there are texts that say God "repented" (Gen. 6:6-8; 1 Sam. 15:11; 2 Sam. 24:16; Joel 2:13-14; John 3:10). Does that mean God changes either in His attributes or His plans? The repentance of God refers to a reversal of God's treatment of particular persons, consequent to their reaction of the treatment. But there is no suggestion that this reaction was not foreseen, or that it took God by surprise and was not provided for in His eternal plan. No change in His eternal purpose is implied when He begins to deal with a person in a new way. His overall plan includes His "repentance" when men respond positively to His warning. For example, when God saw what the Ninevites did and how they turned from their evil ways, God had compassion and did not bring upon them the destruction He had threatened (Jonah 3:10). In this case,

His plan included changing His mind when the population repented of their sins. Such changes do not mean God is mutable.

The Immutability of God and the Doctrine of *Anicca* (Impermanence)

The doctrine of *Anicca* in Buddhism believes that everything is in a state of flux. Nothing is permanent. Everything is impermanent. Let us examine this doctrine.

According to the Scripture, there are some things which are impermanent (1 Cor. 7:31, Psa. 90:6, Isa. 40:6). They are subject to change. But there are others which are permanent. God remains the same (Psa. 102:27, Heb. 1:12). He does not change (Mal. 3:6). *Jesus Christ is the same yesterday and today and forever* (Heb. 13:8). The Word of God is eternal, and it stands firm in the heavens (Psa. 119:89).

If everything is impermanent, the doctrine of *Anicca* is self-contradictory because it too is impermanent. If everything is impermanent, then Nirvana is also impermanent. But Buddhists believe that Nirvana is permanent. If one exception exists in a system of impermanence, is it possible that others may exist too?

Human beings are impermanent, yet Buddhists ask us to look into our hearts to try to eliminate our desires in order to eliminate suffering so that the *samsaric* cycle may be broken thereby achieving Nirvana. The problem is this: How can impermanent beings look inside the impermanent to find the permanent? It is impossible. We can only find permanency in life by looking not inside ourselves (which is subject to change), but to Someone beyond ourselves, and who does not change. There is only one answer: Our immutable God. The impermanent can find the permanent only in the permanent,

> unchanging, immutable God. The *annica* can only find the *nicca* (permanent) in the *Nicca*. Only then can we find real blessedness and meaning of life.

6. **God is holy.** God is absolutely holy, separated from all evil and sin. He is the holy God (Josh. 24:19; 1 Sam. 6:20; Isa. 5:16; 6:3; 1 Peter 1:16; Rev. 4:8), the holy One of Israel (Isa. 5:19, 24; 10:17; 12:6; 17:7; 29:19; 30:11-15; 31:1). Exodus 15:11 reads, *"Who among the gods is like you, O LORD? Who is like you—majestic in holiness, awesome in glory, working wonders?"* God says that God is holy (Lev. 11:44).

   The holiness of God separates Him from sinful humanity (Isa 59:2)[14], and sinners can only approached God through Christ (1 Peter 3:18). We are to be a holy people distinguished by our hatred for sin just as He does (Hab. 1:13), and we are to live holy lives (1 Peter 1:15-16; Eph. 2:1-9).

7. **God is just.** The Lord is just (2 Chron. 12:6). Deuteronomy 32:4 describes God: He is the Rock, His works are perfect, and all His ways are just. A faithful God who does no wrong, upright and just is He. Nehemiah 9:33 says God has been just and has acted faithfully. He is just in His judgments (Rev. 16:5). The Psalmist declares, *"Righteousness and justice are the foundation of your throne; love and faithfulness go before you."* (Psa. 89:14; 97:2)

   Scripture declares, *"The works of his hands are faithful and just"* (Psalm 111:7), and *"everything he does is right and all*

---

[14] There is no recognition of the holiness of God in Hinduism, and therefore no separation exists between men and God. Man is an extension of Brahman.

his ways are just" (Dan. 4:37). We may not completely understand the "justness" of His works because of the injustice around us. But God is sovereign, and when our reasons cannot comprehend His justice, we must bow reverentially outside of faith. Second, we are comforted that God will deal justly with all evil at the end of time (Acts 17:31).

8. **God is love** (1 John 4:8). 1 John 4:9-10 says, *"This is how God showed his love among us: He sent his one and only Son into the world that we might live through him. This is love: not that we loved God, but that he loved us and sent his Son as an atoning sacrifice for our sins."* His love seeks the very best for His objects of love. He wants us to enter into a living relationship with Him. It is a commitment of the will. It is a resolve to seek the best of the other party. His *agape* love is sacrificial. His Son died as an atoning sacrifice for our sins. He seeks the best for us at His own expense.

    The love of God is not only a commitment of the will in seeking the very best for another, it has an emotional element to it. The Bible says that God was distressed because of His love for His people (Isa. 63:9). He grieved over their sins (Gen. 6:6-7; 1 Sam. 15:11, 35; 2 Sam. 24:16; 1 Chron. 21:15; Isa. 63:10; Jer. 42:10; Eze. 6:9).

    His love does not operate independently from His other attributes. All the attributes of God work together. Since God is holy, His love is, therefore, pure. His love is regulated by His holiness. He loves sinners (John 3:16), but hates sin (Hab. 1:13). His love does not set aside His holy requirements.

    His love is regulated also by His justice. Because God is perfectly just, He has to deal with sin, confining the unrepentant to hell. A loving God does not mean He will save everyone as universalism teaches. Universalism teaches love unregulated by justice and holiness, and it contradicts the teaching of Scripture (Mark 9:45-48).

9. **God is gracious.** Grace is underserved kindness. 2 Chronicles 30:9 says, *"God is gracious."* The Psalmist says, *"The Lord is gracious."* (Psa. 111:4, 116:5, 145:8) Joel beseeched the people to return to the Lord because, *"He is gracious and compassionate."* (Joel 2:13) We are justified freely by his grace through the redemption that came by Christ Jesus (Rom. 3:24). Paul says we have God's abundant grace (Rom. 5:17), and he acknowledges that, *"But by the grace of God I am what I am."* (1 Cor. 15:10)

10. **God is good** (Psa. 73:1; 1 Peter 2:3). The Psalmist asks us to *"taste and see that the Lord is good."* (Psa. 34:8) *"The Lord is good and his love endures forever; his faithfulness continues through all generations."* (Psa. 100:5) *"Praise the Lord, for the Lord is good."* (Psa. 135:3) *"The Lord is good to all; he has compassion on all he has made."* (Psa. 145:9) *"Give thanks to the Lord Almighty, for the Lord is good; his love endures forever."* (Jer. 33:11) *"The Lord is good to those whose hope is in him, to the one who seeks him."* (Lam. 3:25) *"The Lord is good, a refuge in times of trouble. He cares for those who trust in him."* (Nah. 1:7)

The Works of God

1. Creation

    a. Immediate creation: God created the heavens and earth, both material and immaterial, without the use of pre-existed materials, intermediary agent/s, or secondary causes. He spoke and the universe came into being (Genesis 1; Neh. 9:6; Isa. 40:26, 42:5, 45:18;

Acts 17:24; Eph. 3:9; Col. 1:16; Rev. 4:11). It was an immediate (instantaneous) and free act of God. He created out of nothing (*ex nihilo*).

b. Mediate creation: God created, shaped, adapted, or transformed existing materials into new creation. For example, the creation of man was not *ex nihilo*. God used the "dust of the ground and breathed into his nostrils the breath of life, and man became a living being." (Gen 2:7) He used one of Adam's ribs to form the woman (Gen 2:21).

God created the universe. It is not evolved over billions of years. Evolution does not answer the question of the "very beginning."

God created the universe. This is not a "random universe" as twentieth-century intellectuals believed. The universe and human life did not come about "by accident, or a by-product of brute, material forces randomly churning over the eons."[15] The eighteenth-century German philosopher Immanuel Kant argued that mechanism can explain everything in the world but two things: beauty and organism. This is called 'the flower problem." If God does not exist, then how do you explain the existence of flowers?[16]

---

[15] Patrick Glynn, *God – The Evidence. The Reconciliation of Faith and Reason in a Postsecular World* (Roseville, CA: Prima Publishing, 1997), p. 23.
[16] Ibid., p. 47.

> **UNFOLDING THE ROSE**[17]
>
> It is only a tiny rosebud,
> A flower of God's design;
> But I cannot unfold the petals
> With these clumsy hands of mine.
>
> The secret of unfolding flowers
> Is not known to such as I.
> God opens this flower so sweetly,
> When in my hands they fade and die.
>
> If I cannot unfold a rosebud,
> This flower of God's design,
> Then how can I think I have wisdom
> To unfold this life of mine?
>
> So I'll trust Him for His leading
> Each moment of every day.
> I will look to Him for His guidance
> Each step of the pilgrim way.
>
> The pathway that lies before me,
> Only my heavenly Father knows.
> I'll trust Him to unfold the moments,
> Just as He unfolds the rose.

God created the universe. It is not the result of the "big bang."[18] The explosion in the universe, which produced millions of pieces of metal cannot assemble themselves into a well-coordinated, designed universe.[19]

---

[17] Author unknown.
[18] The term "big bang" was coined by Fred Hoyle
[19] That was apparently the way Aaron explained the making of the golden calf to Moses. Aaron said the people gave him gold; he threw it into the fire,

God created the universe. The universe is real, not an illusion. Hinduism "suggests that the universe (*brahmand*) is a projection of Brahman. Just as a spider weaves its web, out of itself, so Brahman (the One) throws the *brahmand* (the many) out of itself. The root meaning of the word, *brah* is "to burst forth." The *brahmand* has burst forth out of Brahman. It has emanated out of the being of Brahman. This explanation opens the door for pantheism; for if *brahmand* – the world of the many – is a part and parcel of Brahman, then each unit of the many – stone, a cow, or a man – becomes an object of worship and is considered a god. In order to circumvent this, another equally dominant philosophy of religion (India) maintains that Brahman is only the Real. Its contradictory, not real, the *brahmand* (the universe) is *maya*, illusory, like the illusion of a snake is a rope. What then is this universe? And whence is it? Philosophy of religion (Indian) facing the above dilemma, leaves the question unanswered, stating that the demand for an answer implies the explanation of the inexplicable. This position leaves the enquiring mind perplexed."[20] The doctrine of *maya* does not give the universe any ultimate significance. R. Otto says that the world, "remains ever what it is, a *lila*, a sport of the Deity, a concatenation without goal or end – true, not without objective existence, but eternally worthless, never arriving at a fullness of worth, never glorified and made an abide of the kingdom and of the final dominion of God Himself."[21] The doctrine of creation is something of a stumbling block for Hinduism. It poses a

---

and "bang" ---out came the golden calf (Ex. 32:24). Moses would not believe that!

[20] E. Ahmad-Shah, *Theology – Christian and Hindu* (Lucknow, India: Lucknow Publishing House, 1966), p. 39.

[21] Quoted by Frank Whaling, *An Approach to Dialogue with Hinduism,* p. 68.

dilemma. For Hinduism, "to accept the doctrine of creation would be to do violence to the nature of God as Absolute Being, who cannot be involved in any way in world-life." And yet without it, it is difficult for her to give a doctrinal basis to the values of history or to the goal of history. Otto sums this up thus: "Affirmation of the world is not what he (the Hindu) lacks, but he does lack entirely the positive evaluation of the world, which... belongs inseparably to the essence of Christianity. India gives no genuine worth to the world because it knows nothing of a goal for the world." Later he writes, "in Christianity the creation by God is not derived from the mere idea of absolute dependence, but from the purpose of creation, that it should become the place and scene of the honour of God in "His Kingdom." This area of the fact and purpose of creation is, then, a key one of divergence.[22]

Creation vs. Evolution

In the beginning God created the heavens and earth (Gen. 1:1). The heavens and earth were created. They are not evolved.

Let us make man in our image, in our likeness (Gen. 1:26). The use of the plural pronoun refers the triune-God. Jesus was present at creation. In fact, John declares that *"through him all things were made; without him nothing was made that has been made"* (John 1:3). Colossians 1:16 says that, *"by him all things were created: things in heaven and on earth, visible and invisible, whether thrones or powers or rulers or authorities; all things were created by him and for him."* Hebrews 1:2 also says that *He made the universe.*

---

[22] Ibid., pp. 69-70.

God created each thing *after its kind* (Gen. 1:11, 12, 21, 24, 25). One species does not change into another species. When we refer to evolution, we are not referring to microevolution[23] but to macroevolution, i.e. the change from one species to another species. God created each thing after its own kind. Each kind reproduces after its own kind. One species does not evolve into another species over a long period of time.

The Chicken Egg

A fertilized chicken egg is a very special creation. Before even thinking about a chick developing in an egg, it is interesting to ponder how the chicken manages to get a shell around that slippery, raw, fertilized egg. It is a rare sight on the farm to see raw egg smeared on the outside of the shell. Have you ever attempted to put an egg back into its shell after it rolled off the counter?

The shell itself is highly specialized. Each egg shell has about 10,000 tiny holes or pores. How does that chicken form a shell around a soft, messy egg and design the shell to have porosity? Put a raw egg in warm water and soon you will see tiny bubbles floating up. These bubbles are escaping through the pores in the shell. The developing chick needs these pores to breathe. Evolution requires a need before an organism will change. How does a chicken know it needs to make a shell with porosity, and how can it manufacture such a shell? The chick does not know it needs the holes in the shell to breathe until it dies for lack of air. Of course, dead chicks cannot evolve.

---

[23] That is, genetic variations *within* a certain organism such as different skin colors of people.

Within the first few days after the egg is laid, blood vessels begin to grow out of the developing chick. Two of these attached to the membrane under the eggshell and two attach to the yolk. By the fifth day, the tiny heart is pumping blood through the vessels. What makes those blood vessels grow out of the chick, and how do they know where to go and to what to attached?

The chick feeds from the yolk with the yolk vessels and breathes through the membrane vessels. If any of these vessels do not grow out of the chick or attach to the correct place, the chick will die.

The chick gives off carbon dioxide and water vapor as it metabolizes the yolk. If it does not get rid of the carbon dioxide and water vapor, it will die of gaseous poisoning or drown in its own waste water. These waste products are picked up by the blood vessels and leave through the pores in the eggshell.

By the nineteenth day, the chick is too big to get enough oxygen through the pores in the shell. It must do something or die. How does it know what to do next? By this time, a small tooth called the "egg-tooth" has grown onto its beak. It uses this little tooth to peck a hole into the air sack at the flat end of the egg. When you peel a hard-boiled egg you notice the thin membrane under the shell and the flattened end of the egg. This flattened end, which looks like the hen did not quite fill up her egg shell, is the air sack. The air sack provides only six hours of air for the chick to breathe. Instead of relaxing and breathing deeply, with this new-found supply of air, the chick keeps pecking until it breaks a small hole through the shell to gain access to outside air in adequate amounts.

On the twenty-first day, the chick breaks out of the shell. If one step in the development of the chick is missing or out of order, the chick dies.

> Each step in the development of the chick defies evolutionary logic. The process must be orchestrated by God, our Creator. The impersonal plus time plus chance is not an adequate explanation for the incredible complexities of life as we observe it.[24]

2. Rule

   a. He rules over creation: God rules and has dominion over His creation. The Psalmist declared, *"The Lord is King."* (Psa. 10:16) *"Dominion belongs to the Lord and he rules over the nations."* (Psa. 22:28) *"You rule over the surging sea; when its waves mount up, you still them."* (Psa. 89:9)

   b. He rules over nations: *"May the nations be glad and sing for joy, for you rule the peoples justly and guide the nations of the earth."* (Psa 67:4) Jehoshaphat said, *"O Lord, God of our fathers, are you not the God who is in heaven? You rule over all the kingdoms of the nations. Power and might are in your hand, and no one can withstand you."* (2 Chron 20:6) *"The Most High is sovereign over the kingdoms of men and gives them to anyone he wishes."* (Dan 4:25) He established governmental authority (Rom. 13:1). He rules over the hearts of kings. *"The king's heart is in the hand of the Lord; he directs it like a watercourse wherever he pleases."* (Prov. 21:1) *"He makes nations great, and destroys them; he enlarges nations, and disperses them."* (Job 12:23). *"He rules forever by his power, his eyes watch the nations"* (Psa. 66:7). *"It is God who judges:*

---

[24] The account of the "Chicken Egg" is taken from Jobe Martin, *The Evolution of a Creationist* (Rockwall, TX: Biblical Discipleship Publishers, 1994), pp. 144-46.

He brings one down, he exalts another" (Psa. 75:7 cf. Dan. 4:28-37). He uses nations to accomplish His will (Isa. 7:20, 10:5-15, 45:1-4).

    c.   He rules over men and women: He determined the times set for men and women and the exact places where they should live (Acts 17:26); when they should be promoted or demoted (Psa. 75:7); when they should prosper or perish (1 Sam. 2:6-8); and when they should die (Deut. 32:50, Psa. 104:29).

3. Preservation

    a.   General preservation: God preserves His creation. *"O Lord, you preserve both man and beast."* (Psa. 36:6).

    b.   Special preservation: He preserved Sarah from being taken advantage of by Pharoah (Gen. 12:10-20). He preserved the nation from the evil plan of Haman (Esther). Indeed, *"the Lord preserves the faithful."* (Psa. 31:23) He keeps us in life and does not allow our feet to slip (Psa. 66:9). He preserves the way of His godly ones (Prov. 2:8). He does not forsake His godly ones (Psa. 37:28). He preserves those who came to faith in Jesus (John 10:28).

4. Provision

    a.   Physical provision: He provides sunshine, rain (Matt. 5:45; Gen. 7:12), snow (Isa. 55:10), plants (Jonah 4:6), wind (Prov. 30:4), water (Eze. 17:5-8), etc. He provided manna for His people (Ex. 16). He feeds the birds of the air and clothes the grass of the field. How much more would He take cares of His children? (Matt. 6:25-34)

b. Emotional provision: He provides encouragement (Psa. 10:17, Rom. 15:5; 2 Thess. 2:16). *"So do not fear, for I am with you; do not be dismayed, for I am your God. I will strengthen you and help you; I will uphold you with my righteous right hand."* (Isa. 41:10)

c. Spiritual provision: God gives grace and peace (Rom. 1:7; 1 Cor. 1:3, Eph. 1:2 etc), imparts spiritual gifts (1 Cor. 12:28-31), blesses us with wisdom and understanding (Col. 1:9), and with every spiritual blessing in Christ (Eph. 1:3).

5. Redemption

When Adam and Eve fell, the entire human race was plunged into sin, but God ordained redemption through the Redeemer who was first promised in Genesis 3:15. God subsequently choose Abraham (Gen. 12:1-3) and fulfilled his promise to Abraham through his descendants: Isaac, Jacob, and his 12 sons who gave birth to the nation of Israel. While the history of Israel was marred by continued rebellion, God's redemptive plan was never thwarted. In the fullness of time, the Redeemer, Jesus Christ was born (Gal. 4:4-5) and died for the sins of the world. *"He is the atoning sacrifice for our sins, and not only for ours but also for the sins of the whole world."* (1 John 2:2)

"The majesty and sovereignty of the Lord God Almighty who is from eternity to eternity as the great 'I am that I am' who creates, sustains, controls, redeems and recreates the earth and heavens is completely absent even in the *Rig Veda*."[25]

---

[25] Paul Pillai, *India's Search for the Unknown Christ* (New Delhi: Indian Inland Mission, 1978), p. 193.

6. Judgment

   The Lord is the Judge (Jud. 11:27; Job 9:15). He is the righteous Judge (Psa. 7:11). He is the Judge of the earth (Psa. 94:2, 96:10-13, 98:9). He will judge His people (Deut. 32:36; Psa. 50:4; Heb. 10:30) and the ends of the earth (1 Sam. 2:10, 1 Chron. 16:33; Psa. 82:8). *"God will judge the adulterer and all the sexually immoral."* (Heb. 13:4) *"He will judge the world in righteousness."* (Psa. 9:8)

7. Inspiration

   God inspired the Scriptures. *"All Scripture is God-breathed."* (2 Tim. 3:16)

Applications

1. Our God is worthy of our worship and service. We worship and serve a mighty God.

2. I am comforted by His knowledge of all my needs, sorrows, pain and suffering. There is nothing that will escape His knowledge. If I am being wheeled into the emergency room, He is there. On the other hand, I cannot run away from Him. He is there too!

3. God is infinitely wise and loving. But there are times when I don't understand all His workings. My faith in Him must never be shaken because my finite mind is unable to comprehend the infinite.

4. God is advancing His purpose on earth. I will need to keep in line with His purpose and His program, not my purpose and program. He is building His kingdom. Your Kingdom come. Not "my kingdom come." The

ministry is His ministry, not my ministry of building my own little kingdom on earth.

5. The motivation for my ministry must be the glory and honor of His Name, not my name. His Name is far more important and glorious than my name, or the name of my church, or the name of my denomination, or the name of my organization.

Questions

1. If God is omnipresent, is He also in hell?
2. If God is omniscience, and that He knows my needs, why do we have to pray?
3. Does God create evil according to the KJV of Isaiah 45:7, "I form the light, and create darkness: I make peace, and create evil: I the Lord do all these *things*. (NIV Isaiah 45:7: I form the light and create darkness, I bring prosperity and create disaster; I, the LORD, do all these things)[26].

---

[26] On the surface, this verse appears to give a scriptural basis for the belief that God created evil. Hebrew word *ra'* (translated "evil" in Isa. 45:7) is translated as "adversity" in Ecc. 7:14, and Psa. 94:13. In Isaiah 45, God is differentiating between two opposites with the first pair of things He mentions ("light" and "dark"). To stay consistent, the second pair of things God lists ("peace," **shalom** in Hebrew, and "evil") must also be opposites. The NIV translates *shalom* as "prosperity" (which is a valid translation for *shalom*) and its opposite (*ra'*) as "disaster" Many modern versions translate this phrase more accurately than the *KJV*, as the following examples show: "I make peace and create calamity" (**NKJV**); "I make weal and create woe" (**RSV**); "I make good fortune and create calamity" (**Jerusalem Bible**); "author alike of prosperity and trouble" (**NEB**). One cannot use this verse to accuse God of creating evil.

The Doctrine of Christ (Christology)

Objective

To know Christ and to believe in Him with an unwavering commitment.

The pre-incarnate existence of Christ

1. The testimony of New Testament accounts:

    a. *"No one has ever gone into heaven except the one who came from heaven – the Son of Man."* (John 3:13)
    b. *"The one who comes from above is above all; the one who is from the earth belongs to the earth, and speaks as one from the earth. The one who comes from heaven is above all."* (John 3:31)
    c. *"For I have come down from heaven not to do my will but to do the will of him who sent me."* (John 6:38)

d. *"For the bread of God is he who comes down from heaven and gives life to the world."* (John 6:33 cf. John 6:51, 58)
e. *"What if you see the Son of Man ascend to where he was before!"* (John 6:62)
f. *"But I know him because I am from him and he sent me."* (John 7:29)
g. *"You are from below; I am from above. You are of this world; I am not of this world."* (John 8:23)
h. Jesus said to them, *"If God were your Father, you would love me, for I came from God and now am here. I have not come on my own; but he sent me."* (John 8:42)
i. *"And now, Father, glorify me in your presence with the glory I had with you before the world began."* (John 17:5)
j. *"Father, I want those you have given me to be with me where I am, and to see my glory, the glory you have given me because you loved me before the creation of the world."*(John 17:24)
k. *"For he chose us in him before the creation of the world to be holy and blameless in his sight."* (Eph. 1:4)
l. *"...Christ, a lamb without blemish or defect. He was chosen before the creation of the world..."* (1 Peter 1:19, 20)

2. The Angel of the Lord: The Angel of the Lord (לאָ׳:יהוה‎ Gen. 16:7, 9, 16:11, 22:11, 15; Ex. 3;2; Num. 22:22-35 etc) or the Angel of God ׳מ:לאָ׳ וֹאלהי‎; Gen. 21:17, 31:11; Ex. 14:19; Judg. 6:20, 13:6, 9) in the Old Testament is the visible manifestation (theophany) of the pre-incarnate Christ. The Angel of the Lord and the Angel of God refers to the same person (Judg. 6:20, 21, 13:6-25).

The Identity of the Angel of the Lord

Genesis 16:7-16: The Angel of the Lord found Hagar (Gen. 16:7) and promised her, "I will so increase your descendants that they will be too numerous to count." (Gen. 16:10) A promise which God alone can fulfill. She identifies the Angel as, "The LORD who spoke to her: 'You are the God who sees me,' for she said, 'I have now seen the One who sees me.'" (Gen. 16:13)

Genesis 18: One of the three men (or angels) who visited Abraham to give him the good news of the birth of Isaac is identified as the Lord (Gen. 18:13, 17, 20, 33). He is the Angel of the Lord who visited Abraham.[27]

Genesis 22:1-19: When Abraham was about to kill his son, Isaac, the Angel of the Lord called out to him from heaven (Gen. 22:11), and *"...the angel of the LORD called to Abraham from heaven a second time and said, 'I swear by myself, declares the LORD, that because you have done this and have not withheld your son, your only son, I will surely bless you and make your descendants as numerous as the stars in the sky and as the sand on the seashore. Your descendants will take possession of the cities of their enemies, and through your offspring all nations on earth will be blessed, because you have obeyed me.'"* The Angel of the Lord said, "I swear by myself." There is no greater person by whom He could swear. The Angel of the Lord is the Lord Himself.

Genesis 32:24-32: The "man" (or more specifically the Angel of the Lord cf. Hos. 12:4) who wrestled with Jacob was identified as God (Gen. 32:28, 30).

Exodus 3:1-22: The Angel of the Lord appeared to Moses in flames of fire from within a bush (Ex. 3:2). Then when Moses turned to look at the burning bush, Exodus 3:4-7 records, *"When the LORD saw that he had gone over to look, God called to him from within the bush, 'Moses! Moses!' And Moses said, 'Here I am.' 'Do not come any closer,' God said.*

---

[27] The other "two angels" visited Lot in Genesis 18:22, 19:1. The "man" who wrestled with Jacob was probably the Angel of the Lord (Gen. 32:24-32).

'Take off your sandals, for the place where you are standing is holy ground. Then he said, 'I am the God of your father, the God of Abraham, the God of Isaac and the God of Jacob.' At this, Moses hid his face, because he was afraid to look at God. The LORD said, 'I have indeed seen the misery of my people in Egypt. I have heard them crying out because of their slave drivers, and I am concerned about their suffering....'' The Angel of the Lord is identified as the Lord (יהוה), God (הואלהי), and "I AM WHO I AM" (Ex. 3:14).

Numbers 22:22-35: When Balaam was going to curse Israel, the Angel of the Lord who intercepted him was identified as the Lord (Num. 22:28, 31). *But God was very angry when he went, and the angel of the LORD stood in the road to oppose him. Balaam was riding on his donkey, and his two servants were with him. When the donkey saw the angel of the LORD standing in the road with a drawn sword in his hand, she turned off the road into a field. Balaam beat her to get her back on the road. Then the angel of the LORD stood in a narrow path between two vineyards, with walls on both sides. When the donkey saw the angel of the LORD, she pressed close to the wall, crushing Balaam's foot against it. So he beat her again. Then the angel of the LORD moved on ahead and stood in a narrow place where there was no room to turn, either to the right or to the left. When the donkey saw the angel of the LORD, she lay down under Balaam, and he was angry and beat her with his staff. Then the LORD opened the donkey's mouth, and she said to Balaam, "What have I done to you to make you beat me these three times?" Balaam answered the donkey, "You have made a fool of me! If I had a sword in my hand, I would kill you right now." The donkey said to Balaam, "Am I not your own donkey, which you have always ridden, to this day? Have I been in the habit of doing this to you?" "No," he said. Then the LORD opened Balaam's eyes, and he saw the angel of the LORD standing in the road with his sword drawn. So he bowed low and fell face down. The angel of the LORD asked him, "Why have you beaten your donkey these three times? I have come here to oppose you because your path is a reckless one before me. The donkey saw me and turned away from me these three times. If she had not turned away, I would certainly have killed you by now, but I would have spared her." Balaam said to the angel of the LORD, "I have sinned. I did not realize you were standing in the road to oppose me. Now if you are displeased, I will go back." The angel of the LORD said to Balaam, "Go with the men, but speak only what I tell you." So Balaam went with the princes of Balak.*

Judges 2:1-5: The Angel of the Lord was identified as the One who brought the Israelites out of Egypt, and promised to fulfill His covenant. The people understood the Angel of the Lord to be the Lord Himself, and hence "they offered sacrifices to the Lord." *The angel of the LORD went up from Gilgal to Bokim and said, "I brought you up out of Egypt and led you into the land that I swore to give to your forefathers. I said, 'I will never break my covenant with you, and you shall not make a covenant with the people of this land, but you shall break down their altars.' Yet you have disobeyed me. Why have you done this? Now therefore I tell you that I will not drive them out before you; they will be thorns in your sides and their gods will be a snare to you." When the angel of the LORD had spoken these things to all the Israelites, the people wept aloud, and they called that place Bokim. There they offered sacrifices to the LORD.*

The Angel of the Lord was identified as the Angel of God (Judges 13:9), the Lord (Judges 5:23, 6:11-24; 13:3-21; 2 Sam. 24:16-25; 1Kings 19:7-15; 2 Kings 1;3-18; 1 Chron. 21:12-30; Psa. 34, 35, Zech. 3:1-10), God (Gen. 21:17; 31:11-13; Judges 13:9, 22).

The Distinction from Jehovah

The Angel of the Lord is distinct from Jehovah God because:

    a. He was sent by the Lord to deliver Israel. Numbers 20:15-16: *"Our forefathers went down into Egypt, and we lived there many years. The Egyptians mistreated us and our fathers, but when we cried out to the LORD, he heard our cry and sent an angel and brought us out of Egypt. Now we are here at Kadesh, a town on the edge of your territory."* That the angel who was sent by the Lord was the Angel of the Lord is clear from Exodus 14:19. Similarly, Isaiah 63:7-9 proclaims, *"I will tell of the kindnesses of the LORD, the deeds for which he is to be praised, according to all the LORD has done for us-- yes, the many good things he has done for the house of Israel, according to his compassion and many kindnesses. He said, 'Surely they are my people, sons who will not be false to me'; and so he became their Savior. In all their distress he too was distressed, and the angel of his presence saved them. In his love and mercy he redeemed them; he lifted them up and carried them all the days of old.'"*

    b. He was sent to protect His people. Daniel 3:25-28: The identity of the fourth person who looked "like a son of the gods" (Dan. 3:25) was not identified as the Angel of the Lord, but most probably He is the pre-incarnate Christ. He was identified simply as the "angel" (Dan. 3:28).

    He was sent to guard His people into the promise land in Exodus 23:20-23: *"See, I am sending an angel ahead of you to guard you along the way and to bring you to the place I have prepared.*

Pay attention to him and listen to what he says. Do not rebel against him; he will not forgive your rebellion, since my Name is in him. If you listen carefully to what he says and do all that I say, I will be an enemy to your enemies and will oppose those who oppose you. My angel will go ahead of you and bring you into the land of the Amorites, Hittites, Perizzites, Canaanites, Hivites and Jebusites, and I will wipe them out." God said that His Name is in Him. The angel, therefore, was probably the Angel of the Lord.

The angel in Exodus 32:33-34 was probably the Angel of the Lord. *The LORD replied to Moses, "Whoever has sinned against me I will blot out of my book. Now go, lead the people to the place I spoke of, and my angel will go before you. However, when the time comes for me to punish, I will punish them for their sin."* Exodus 33:2: *"I will send an angel before you and drive out the Canaanites, Amorites, Hittites, Perizzites, Hivites and Jebusites."*

c. The Angel of the Lord was sent to execute judgment. When Satan rose up against Israel and incited David to take a census, God was displeased, and sent the Angel of the Lord to execute judgment upon the nation (1 Chron. 21:1-30).

d. The Angel of the Lord prayed to Jehovah. The Angel of the Lord prayed to the Lord Almighty in Zechariah 1:11-13: *And they reported to the angel of the LORD, who was standing among the myrtle trees, "We have gone throughout the earth and found the whole world at rest and in peace." Then the angel of the LORD said, "LORD Almighty, how long will you withhold mercy from Jerusalem and from the* towns of Judah, which you have been angry with these seventy years?" So the LORD spoke kind and comforting words to the angel who talked with me.

e. The Angel of the Lord rebuked Satan using the name "Lord" in Zechariah 3:1-10: *Then he showed me Joshua the high priest standing before the angel of the LORD, and Satan standing at his right side to accuse him. The LORD said to Satan, "The LORD rebuke you, Satan! The LORD, who has chosen Jerusalem, rebuke you! Is not this man a burning stick snatched from the fire?" Now Joshua was dressed in filthy clothes as he stood before the angel. The angel said to those who were standing before him, "Take off his filthy clothes." Then he said to Joshua, "See, I have taken away your sin, and I will put rich garments on you." Then I said, "Put a clean turban on his head." So they put a clean turban on his head and clothed him, while the angel of the LORD stood by. The angel of the LORD gave this charge to Joshua: "This is what the LORD Almighty says: 'If you will walk in my ways and keep my requirements, then you will govern my house and have charge of my courts, and I will give you a place among these standing here. Listen, O high priest Joshua and your associates seated before you, who are men symbolic of things to come: I am going to bring my servant, the Branch. See, the stone I have set in front of Joshua! There are seven eyes on that one stone, and I will engrave an inscription on it,' says the LORD Almighty, 'and I will remove the sin of this land in a single day. 'In that day each of you will invite his neighbor to sit under his vine and fig tree,' declares the LORD Almighty.*

C. Fred Dickason concludes, there are four considerations that help to identify the Angel of Jehovah as Christ in pre-incarnate appearances. (1)

The second person of the Trinity, the Son, is the visible God of the New Testament (Jn 1:14, 18; Col 2:8-9). Accordingly, the Son was the visible manifestation of God in the Old Testament also. (2) The Angel of Jehovah no longer appeared after Christ's incarnation. A reference such as Matthew 1:20 does not identify the angel and should be understood as an angel of the Lord. (3) They both were sent by God and had similar ministries such as revealing, guiding and judging. The Father was never sent. (4) This angel could not be the Father or the Spirit. They never take bodily form (Jn 1:18; 3:8). The Angel of Jehovah, then, according to all the evidence, seems to be the pre-incarnate Son. His appearances evidence His eternal existence.[28]

The Virgin Birth of Christ

Christ was born of the Virgin Mary (Isa. 7:14; Matt. 1:18, 23; Luke 1:27, 34). The virgin birth kept Jesus from receiving a sin nature from either Joseph or Mary, and therefore He was the sinless Lamb of God qualified to be the Redeemer of sinful humanity.

---

[28] C. Fred Dickason, *Angels, Elect and Evil* (Chicago, IL: Moody Press, 1975), pp. 80-81. Frank Whaling says that the two most popular Hindu *avataras*, Krishna and Rama "made no claim to divinity, and were not claimed to be divine until long after their death. As mythological legends slowly grew around them, in the process of time they came to be worshipped as divine. Professor D. D. Kosambi sums this idea up, 'Krishna, then, is not a single historical figure but compounded of many semi-legendary heroes who helped in the formation of a new food-producing society. The work was done from 800 B.C. onwards. When Heliodorus dedicated his pillar, Balarama and other Yadu heroes still received equal honour with Krishna in Shunga sculptures. But by the fourth century B.C. the Gita had been composed and Krishna grew to new heights as the fountain-head of religious philosophy, inspiration to leading Indian thinkers from Samkara to Mahatma Gandhi.'" (Frank Whaling, *An Approach to Dialogue with Hinduism*, p. 59.)

The virgin birth is directly related to the uniqueness (deity) and sinlessness of Christ. He was called "the Holy one of God" (John 6:69). If Jesus had not been born of a virgin, totally separate from the seed and inherited sin of Adam, then He could not have been sinless and fulfilled His mission of saving us from our sins (Matt. 1:21, Romans 5:12). Jesus bypassed the curse of sin and the curse of Jeconiah to be the sinless Lamb of God.

The Deity of Christ[29]

1. The explicit claims of New Testament writers:

    a. John 1:1: *In the beginning was (eivmi, imperfect) the Word, and the Word was with God and the Word was God; (cf. John.1:14) the Word became flesh and made his dwelling among us. We have seen his glory, the glory of the One and Only, who came from the Father, full of grace and truth.*

    b. John 20:28: *Thomas said to him, "My Lord and my God!"* Jesus did not reject the designation "God" used by Thomas.

    c. Romans 9:5: *Christ, who is God over all, forever praised! Amen.*

    d. Phil. 2:6: *Who, being in very nature God, did not consider equality with God something to be grasped.*

---

[29] The Doctrine of the Deity of Christ is opposed to: (i) Docetism - Jesus was truly spirit and only appeared to be a man. (ii) Gnosticism - Jesus was only a man taken over by the heavenly Christ which never became incarnate. The heavenly Christ returned to heaven before the crucifixion. (iii) Arianism - Jesus was created slightly lower than God. Then Jesus created all things.

e. Titus 2:13: *While we wait for the blessed hope – the glorious appearing of our great God and Savior, Jesus Christ.*

2. The claims of Christ point to divinity:

   a. *Jesus claimed, "I and the Father are one."* (John 10:30) The Jews understood His claim to deity, and sought to kill Him (cf. John 5:18).

   b. Jesus claimed He was the Christ, the Son of God, in Matthew 26:63-64 when He answered the question by the high priest. The high priest considered His claim blasphemous. It would not have been blasphemous if the high priest didn't understand His claim of deity. The title "Son of God" was understood by Jesus' contemporaries as identifying Himself as God, and equal with the Father.

3. The works of Christ, which only God can perform, substantiate His deity.

   a. **Forgiveness of sins** (Mark 2:1-12). When Jesus forgave the sins of the paralytic, some teachers of the law considered His claim to forgive sins a blasphemy against God because only God can forgive sins. The Scriptures say He forgives sins (Col 3:13; 1 John 1:9).[30]

---

[30] The forgiveness that the *bhakta* finds from the Hindu *avatar* is a kind of indulgence, "an overlooking of the fault, out of compassion for the suffering, which the faulty one has drawn upon himself." The best of the *avatars* are impressive indeed. For example, it was said of Rama that, "From the love that he bore his followers, Rama took the form of a man, and by himself enduring misery secured their happiness." But with even the best of the Hindu *avatars* there is no cross, no Golgotha, no expiation. There is no sense of their suffering, or dying, or agonizing for man. They neither

b. **Resurrection of the dead.** Jesus raised Lazarus from the dead (John 11) and brought back to life the daughter of a ruler (Matt. 9:18-25). Jesus claimed, *"...the dead will hear the voice of the Son of God and those who hear will live. For as the Father has life in himself, so he has granted the Son to have life in himself."* (John 5:25-26) The power to give life to the dead is the power of God Himself. No one else has the power to give life except God.

c. **Judgment of the world.** Jesus has been given the authority to judge the world (John 5:22, 27). The Apostle Peter preached that He *"...is the one whom God appointed as judge of the living and the dead."* (Acts 10:42) Paul also said that Jesus will judge the world (Acts 17:31), and that *"...God will judge men's secrets through Jesus Christ."* (Rom. 2:16) *"He will bring to light what is hidden in darkness and will expose the motives of men's hearts."* (1 Cor. 4:5) Paul wrote in 2 Timothy 4:1: *"In the presence of God and of Christ Jesus, who will judge the living and the dead,"* (cf. 1 Peter 4:5) is a clear reference to the deity of Jesus as He was

---

offer full salvation to man, nor do they fully reveal God. They have arisen in order to fill a vacuum in the soul of Hinduism that could not be satisfied in other ways. Hinduism has not given sufficient thought to the revolutionary significance for the world of the fact that God became man, because the traffic of *avatars* is so common as to convey no challenge such as we encounter in the Follow me of Jesus Christ. The Hindu *avatar* is a temporary intervention in the affairs of mankind on the part of the divine that can be repeated in different forms when it becomes necessary. In fact, there are doubts about the actual historicity of the two most popular *avataras,* namely Krishna and Rama. It is significant that they are popular because they represent the desire of mortal man to see God come down from the top of His castle in eternity in order to share in the common life of the human race. (Frank Whaling, *An Approach to Dialogue with Hinduism,* p. 58). In Dr. Radhakrishnan's index of his edition of the *Brahma Sutra* there is no mention of the word, "Forgiveness." (Ibid., p. 61.).

given the power to judge equal to that of God the Father. The prerogative to judge the world is that of God Himself (Heb. 10:30, 13:4; James 4:12). The same prerogative has been given to Christ. All nations will be gathered before Him for judgment (Matt. 25:31-46, Rev. 20:11).

    d. **Creation.** *"Through him all things were made; without him nothing was made that has been made."* (John 1:3) *"The world was made through him."* (John 1:10) *"For by him all things were created: things in heaven and on earth, visible and invisible, whether thrones or powers or rulers or authorities; all things were created by him and for him."* (Col. 1:16) *"But in these last days he has spoken to us by his Son, whom he appointed heir of all things, and through whom he made the universe."* (Heb. 1:2) *"In the beginning, O Lord, you laid the foundations of the earth, and the heavens are the work of your hands."* (Heb. 1:10)

    e. **Sustaining the universe.** *"In him all things hold together."* (Col 1:17) He sustains all things by the power of His word (Heb 1:3).

    f. **Dissolving and recreating the universe.** He will dissolve this present earth and make everything new (Rev. 21:5).

4. The divine attributes ascribed to Jesus. *"For in Christ all the fullness of the Deity lives in bodily form."* (Col 2:9)

    a. **Omniscience.** Jesus knew all people, and He knew what is in a person (John 2:24-25). He knows all things (John 16:30). *"Jesus had known from the beginning which of them did not believe and who would betray him."* (John 6:64) He knew who was going to betray Him (John 13:11). He knew the evil thoughts of man (Matt 9:4). He is the One who searches the minds and hearts (Rev. 2:23).

b. **Omnipresence.** *"He is not far from each one of us."* (Acts 17:27) He promised He will be with us to the very end of the age (Matt. 28:20), and where two or three come together in His Name (Matt 18:20).

c. **Omnipotence.** He was able to calm the storm (Matt 8:25-26). *"He is able to save completely those who come to God through him."* (Heb 7:25) He is the Almighty (Rev. 1:8).

d. **Immutability.** He is the same yesterday and today and forever (Heb. 13:8).

e. **Sovereignty.** God has given Jesus all authority (Matt. 28:18). He is over all (Rom. 9:5). He is the Ruler of the kings of the earth (Rev. 1:5). Angels, authorities and powers are in submission to Him (1 Peter 3:22). He is both "Lord and Christ" (Acts 2:36). *God exalted him to the highest place and gave him the name that is above every name, that at the name of Jesus every knee should bow, in heaven and on earth and under the earth, and every tongue confess that Jesus Christ is Lord, to the glory of God the Father.* (Phil 2:9-11) *In everything he might have the supremacy.* (Col. 1:18) He is "exalted above the heavens" (Heb 7:26). He is Lord of lords and King of kings (Rev. 17:14, 19:16).

f. **Eternity**[31]. Micah (5:2) prophesized that His origin was from days of eternity. He is the Eternal Father (Isa. 9:6). John1:1: *In the beginning was (eivmi, imperfect) the Word, and the Word was with God and the*

---

[31] See the section on the *Pre-existence of Christ* which also gives evidences of His eternity.

Word was God. Jesus said, *"Before Abraham was born, I am!"* (John 8:58) *He is before all things.* (Col 1:17) *"I am the Alpha and the Omega, the First and the Last, the Beginning and the End."* (Rev. 1:8; 21:6, 22:13) *God ...chose us in him before the creation of the world to be holy and blameless in his sight.* (Eph. 1:4) Jude 25 praised *"to the only God our Savior be glory, majesty, power and authority, through Jesus Christ our Lord, before all ages, now and forevermore! Amen."*

    g. **Holy.** Jesus is the Holy and Righteous One (Acts 3:14). He is holy and true (Rev. 3:7). He *"is holy, blameless, pure, set apart from sinners, exalted above the heavens."* (Heb 7:26)

5. The titles of Christ's divinity:

    a. Yahweh, יְהֹוָה translated kurios (κύριος) in the New Testament (Zech.12:10b; cf. Rev. 1:7; Psa. 68:18; cf. Eph. 4:8-10; Psa. 102:12; cf. Heb. 1:10,11; Isa.6:5; cf. John 12:41; Jer. 23:5,6; cf. 1 Cor. 1:30; Matt. 3:1; cf. Matt. 12:6; 21:12,13 [*Lord of the temple*]; Matt. 12:8 [*Lord of the Sabbath*]).

    b. Adonai, אֲדוֹן translated kurios in the NT (Psa. 110:1; cf. Matt. 22:44 and Mk. 12:36; Lk. 10:43; Acts 2:34, 35; Heb. 1:13; 10:13).

    c. Elohim, אֱלֹהִים translated Theos (θεός) in the NT. In Isaiah 40:3, Christ is spoken of as both Yahweh and Elohim (cf. Luke 3:6).

The sinlessness of Christ

Jesus Christ is sinless. He is *the Holy and Righteous One* (Acts 3:14). He is the *"lamb without blemish or defect."* (1 Pet. 1:19) *"He committed no sin, and no deceit was found in his mouth."* (1 Pet. 2:22) *"In him is no sin."* (1 John 3:5) He *"was without sin."* (Heb. 4:15) He *"is holy, blameless, pure, set apart from sinners, exalted above the heavens."* (Heb. 7:26) No one convicts Him of sin (John 8:46).

If Jesus Christ is blemished, having sin, He could not have been a perfect sacrifice demanded by God to atone for the sins of the world, typified by the Old Testament Passover (Ex. 12:5, Lev. 23:12), and fulfilled by Christ, the Passover Lamb (1 Cor. 5:7). The sinlessness of Christ is an absolute prerequisite to His work of substitution on the cross.

The impeccability of Christ

Jesus Christ is impeccable, meaning He *cannot* sin, or He *could not have* sinned. The *impeccability* of Christ means His *impossibility* to sin, even though Christ has a "peccable" human nature. Jesus Christ has a "peccable" human nature, but He is an impeccable *Person,* and therefore He could not have sinned. "If the human nature had been unsustained as in the case of Adam by a divine nature, it is clear that the human nature of Christ might have sinned. This possibility, however, is completely removed by the presence of the divine nature."[32]

If Christ is an impeccable Person, could He then be tempted just as we are (Heb. 4:15)? Does temptability presuppose susceptibility to sin? John Walvoord explains,

> It is possible for a rowboat to attack a battleship, even though it is conceivably impossible for the rowboat to conquer the battleship. The idea that temptability implies susceptibility is unsound. While the temptation may be real, there may be infinite power to resist that temptation and if this power is infinite, the person is impeccable.[33]

---

[32] John F. Walvoord, *Jesus Christ Our Lord* (Chicago, IL: Moody Press, 1969), p. 149.
[33] Ibid., p. 147.

The temptations experienced by Christ are real in every aspect, but He is impeccable, and He could not have sinned.

The Kenosis of Christ

The *kenosis* of Christ, according to Philippians 2:6-11, means Christ left His pre-incarnate position to take on a servant-humanity.[34]

Several clarifications:

1. Christ did not give up or lay aside His deity at His incarnation. He did not cease to be God at His incarnation. Christ possessed the very nature of God, and was equal with God. The translated Greek present tense of the verb "existed" (NASB) or "being" (NIV) points to the Lord's continuing existence with the full nature of God. At the incarnation, Jesus adopted a form of existence (God-man) that was different from His Father's, but His "equality with God" was always His. He did not need to grasp after equality with God because He already possessed it.

2. Christ did not give up His dependence on His Father. The Son was always dependent on the Father, and He never acted independently of His Father.

3. At the incarnation and during His earthly ministry, Christ voluntarily restricted the use of some of His attributes. He was omnipotent, but He also possessed the power of self-limitation. He laid aside the freedom afforded Him during His former existence due to the limitations present in a human body.

---

[34] Charles C. Ryrie, *Basic Theology* (Wheaton, IL: Victor Books, 1986), p. 262.

4. When Christ took on the very nature of a servant, it did not mean, however, that He inherited the sinful nature of man. He was without sin (Heb. 4:15). The phrase "the very nature of a servant" is intended to demonstrate His humiliation. He was willing to change His form of existence for the sake of saving the world. He was willing to humble "Himself and became obedient to death—even death on a cross!"

The Humanity of Christ

Jesus had two natures in one person. He was not half God and half man. He was both Human and Divine. He was completely God and completely man (Hypostatic Union)[35]. Colossians 2:9: *"For in Christ all the fullness of the Deity lives in bodily form."* In Philippians 2:5-7: *"...Christ Jesus: Who, being in very nature God, did not consider equality with God something to be grasped, but made himself nothing, taking the very nature of a servant, being made in human likeness."*

Christ was fully human:

- He had a human body (Matt. 27:58-64)
- He learned (Luke 2:46)
- He could be touched (1 John 1:1)
- He was born of a woman (Gal. 4:4)
- His body grew (Luke 2:52)
- He was tempted (Matt. 4:1; Mark 1:13; Luke 4:2; Heb. 2:18, 4:15)

---

[35]The Hypostatic Union is opposed to: (i) Eutychianism - The two natures of Jesus are completely 'mixed' and undiscernible. (ii) Nestorianism - The two natures are not in contact with each other. (iii) Monophycitism - The two natures combined and became one, a new type of being. Then Jesus would be neither God nor man, but a third something.

- He was hungry (Matt. 4:2, 21:18, 25:35-44; Mark 11:12; Luke 4:2)
- He ate food (Matt. 9:10; Luke 24:43)
- He wept (Luke 19:42; John 11:39)
- He was thirsty (Matt. 25:35-44; John 19:28)
- He felt tired (John 4:6)
- He slept (Matt. 8:24; Mark 4:38; Luke 8:23)
- He had a human spirit (Matt. 26:38; Luke 23:46)
- He died (Matt. 27:50)

The Death of Christ

The death of Jesus Christ is unique, different from all other deaths of the world. His death accomplished what no one else could accomplish. The deaths of some people have left an imprint on the world—for example, the deaths of Gandhi, Abraham Lincoln and John F. Kennedy. But if you were to probe further on what they accomplished through their deaths, you would be hard pressed to come up with a good answer. No doubt, we all agree the world is different because they contributed much to society, but when they died, they just died. Their hearts stop beating and they were ushered into eternity. But when we consider the death of Jesus, there are several unique accomplishments on the Cross. Jesus accomplished "certain things" at His death. What are these accomplishments?

1. Propitiation of sins: At His death, Christ became the atoning sacrifice for our sins. The NASB translates the word ἱλασμός in 1 John 2:2 and 4:10 as "propitiation," meaning the wrath of God was turned away from us because Christ bore on Himself the sins of the world. The wrath of God should rightfully rest upon fallen humanity, but the death of Christ turned that wrath away so that it is now possible for us to be redeemed men and women.

2. Redemption of sinners: By His death on the Cross, Christ paid the penalty of sin so sinful men and women could be redeemed. He accomplished the redemption of sinners through His death. He paid the ransom. He gave Himself as a ransom for all (Matt. 20:28; 1 Tim. 2:6). Because of His death, the world is now redeemable. This does not mean everybody is now saved, but it means everyone is redeemable. Whoever believes in the Name of Jesus Christ will be redeemed from their sin into life eternal.

3. Reconciliation to God: Jesus' death brought about reconciliation of the world, i.e the position of the world was changed so everyone could be reconciled to God (2 Cor. 5:18-19).

4. Substitution of sinners: Christ died in the place of sinners (2 Cor. 5:21). The penalty of sins is death, eternal separation from God. But Jesus took our place and paid the penalty so we could be freed from the chains of eternal punishment. That gift of salvation is available for everyone.

5. Creation of "one new man" (Eph. 2:15). The death of Jesus fulfilled all the demands of the Mosaic Law, and destroyed the dividing wall[36] of hostility between Jews and Gentiles (Eph. 2:14), thereby creating one new man, the church (Eph. 2:6). God deals with both believing Jews and believing Gentiles now equally as Christians.

---

[36] Qin Shi Huang, the first emperor of China built the *wall* of China. The wall was meant to keep enemies out. It is a wall of hostility. But there is a greater spiritual wall of hostility between Jews and gentiles. Jesus, instead of building the wall, destroyed it so that both Jews and Gentiles become one new man in God. Emperor Qin left China with a wall, a tomb and a name. Jesus left the world with a bridge (to God), an empty tomb, and a Name above all names.

Islam's view of Jesus Christ

1. Islam, like the ancient heresy, Docetism, believes Jesus did not die; He merely appeared to do so. Unlike Docetism, which believed that Jesus was God who took on the appearance of a human being, Islam denies the divinity of Jesus all together. It is a further perversion of Docetism.

   According to Sura 4:156ff, "The Jews say, 'Verily we have killed the Messiah, Jesus the Son of Mary, the Apostle of God,' but he was neither killed nor crucified by them; he merely appeared so to them... Really, indeed, they did not kill him, but God took him up to Himself."

   The Nestorians believed that only the human Christ (not the divine Christ) died. Since Islam denies the divinity of Christ, the expression in Sura 4.157 changed the Nestorian belief and further altered the doctrine to deny the human death of Christ altogether.

2. Arius taught (c.318) that God created, before all things, a Son who was the first creature, but who was neither equal to nor co-eternal with the Father. Like Arianism, Islam believes Jesus was a mere man; not divine. He is highly respected as the second-last prophet, but Islam advanced the Arian heresy by refusing the use the designation, "The Son of God" when referring to Jesus. To Muslims, it is blasphemy to speak of Jesus as the Son.

   The following verses from the Koran testified to their belief about Jesus:

   > *O People of the Book [Christians and Jews]! Commit no excesses in your religion: Nor say of God aught but the truth. Christ Jesus the son of Mary was (no more than) a messenger of God, and His Word, which He bestowed on Mary, and a spirit proceeding from Him: so believe in God and His*

messengers. Say not "Trinity" : desist: it will be better for you: for God is one God: Glory be to Him: (far exalted is He) above having a son. Quran 4:171

Christ the son of Mary was no more than a messenger; many were the messengers that passed away before him. His mother was a woman of truth. They had both to eat their (daily) food. Quran 5:75

[Jesus] said: Surely I am a servant of God; He has given me the Book and made me a prophet. Quran 19:30

In blasphemy indeed are those that say that God is Christ the son of Mary. Quran 5:17

They do blaspheme who say: "God is Christ the son of Mary." But said Christ: "O Children of Israel! worship God, my Lord and your Lord." Quran 5:72

And behold! God will say: "O Jesus the son of Mary! Didst thou say unto men, worship me and my mother as gods in derogation of God?" He will say: "Glory to Thee! Never could I say what I had no right (to say)." Quran 5:116

The Resurrection of Christ

1. Prophecies of the Old Testament

The resurrection of Christ is a fulfillment of Old Testament prophecies:

Therefore, my heart is glad and my tongue rejoices; my body also will rest secure, because you will not abandon me to the grave, nor will you let your Holy One see decay. You have made known to me the path of life; you will fill me with joy in your presence, with eternal pleasures at your right hand. (Psalm 16:9-11)

The LORD says to my Lord: "Sit at my right hand until I make your enemies a footstool for your feet." The LORD will extend your mighty scepter from Zion; you will rule in the midst of your enemies. Your troops will be willing on your day of battle. Arrayed in holy majesty, from the womb of the dawn you will receive the dew of your youth. The LORD has sworn and will not change his mind: "You are a priest forever, in the order of Melchizedek." The Lord is at your right hand; he will crush kings on the day of his wrath. He will judge the nations, heaping up the dead and crushing the rulers of the whole earth. He will drink from a brook beside the way; therefore he will lift up his head. (Psalm 110:1-7)

He was assigned a grave with the wicked, and with the rich in his death, though he had done no violence, nor was any deceit in his mouth. Yet it was the LORD's will to crush him and cause him to suffer, and though the LORD makes his life a guilt offering, he will see his offspring and prolong his days, and the will of the LORD will prosper in his hand. After the suffering of his soul, he will see the light of life and be satisfied; by his knowledge my righteous servant will justify many, and he will bear their iniquities. Therefore I will give him a portion among the great, and he will divide the spoils with the strong, because he poured out his life unto death, and was numbered with the transgressors. For he bore the sin of many, and made intercession for the transgressors. (Isaiah 53:9-12)

2. Prophecies of Christ Himself

Christ prophesized His own death and resurrection:

Jesus answered them, "Destroy this temple, and I will raise it again in three days." The Jews replied, "It has taken 46 years to build this temple, and you are going to raise it in three days?" But the temple he had spoken of was his body. After he was raised from the dead, his disciples recalled what he had said. Then they believed the Scripture and the words that Jesus had spoken. (John 2:19-22)

Then some of the Pharisees and teachers of the law said to him, "Teacher, we want to see a miraculous sign from you." He answered, "A wicked and adulterous generation asks for a miraculous sign! But none will be given it except the sign of the prophet Jonah. For as Jonah was three days and three nights in the belly of a huge fish, so the Son of Man will be three days and three nights in the heart of the earth." (Matthew 12:38-40)

When they came together in Galilee, he said to them, "The Son of Man is going to be betrayed into the hands of men. They will kill him, and on the third day he will be raised to life." And the disciples were filled with grief. (Matthew 17:22-23)

Now as Jesus was going up to Jerusalem, he took the 12 disciples aside and said to them, "We are going up to Jerusalem, and the Son of Man will be betrayed to the chief priests and the teachers of the law. They will condemn him to death and will turn him over to the Gentiles to be mocked and flogged and crucified. On the third day he will be raised to life!" (Matthew 20:17-19)

Then Jesus told them, "This very night you will all fall away on account of me, for it is written: 'I will strike the shepherd, and the sheep of the flock will be scattered.' But after I have risen, I will go ahead of you into Galilee." (Matthew 26:31-32)

The reason my Father loves me is that I lay down my life — only to take it up again. No one takes it from me, but I lay it down of my own accord. I have authority to lay it down and authority to take it up again. This command I received from my Father." (John 10:17-18)

3. Evidences of His Resurrection

   a. The broken Roman seal. The Roman guards affixed the Roman seal on the tomb to prevent any attempt at opening it. Anyone who broke the seal or failed in his duty would receive the death sentence. The guard (κουστωδίαν· Matt. 27:65) of soldiers consisted of four to 16 men (four men per shift while the others slept in front of whatever was being guarded).

   The Roman seal symbolized the power of the Roman Empire. Unfortunately, the power to seal the tomb had no power to keep Jesus inside. The seal was broken by a greater Power—His power. After all, He is the One who has *all* authority, both in heaven and on earth. Matthew 28:2 says that, *"There was a violent earthquake, for an angel of the Lord came down from heaven and, going to the tomb, rolled back the stone and sat on it."*

   The Roman guards were fearful for their lives because they knew they could expect execution by the Roman Emperor if they failed in their duty. Therefore, they were *"so afraid of him that they shook and became like dead men."* (Matthew 28:4) The guards would not have fallen asleep (Matthew 28:13) and failed in their duty, knowing their heads would be placed on the chopping board. The disciples did not steal Jesus' body. He rose from the dead. The resurrection is an irrefutable fact.

   b. The stone was removed. It is estimated that the stone, which was rolled onto the entrance of the tomb, weighed approximately two tons.[37] The stone was rolled *down a slope* to seal the entrance of the tomb. It would be preset with a wedge and then rolled into place by removing the

---

[37] λίθος μέγας (Matt. 27.60) —a great stone. μέγας σφόδρα (Mk. 16.4) — extremely large.

wedge. But the extremely heavy stone had been rolled *up a slope* away from the entrance of the tomb, in fact, away from the entire massive sepulcher.[38] The disciples (who were extremely fearful of the Jews because their Master had died) would never have been able to perform such a feat! It was also impossible for anyone to roll the stone away from *inside* the tomb because there was no "door handle" on the inside. If there had been a door handle on the inside, the sheer weight of the stone and its position would have made it impossible to roll away. The stone had to be picked up and dumped away from the entrance by the power of the Almighty.

c. The empty tomb. The tomb was empty. It has been proposed that the women and the disciples went to the wrong tomb. This theory can be easily dismissed because the chief priests and the Roman guards could have easily produced the body of Jesus from the right tomb, therefore, dismissing the disciples' claim of His resurrection. But they couldn't produce a body. The disciples and the women went to the right tomb and found it empty. Christ is risen.

d. The grave clothes. John bent over the entrance of the tomb and looked in, seeing the strips of linen lying inside the tomb. Peter, on the other hand, went into the tomb and saw the strips of linen lying there along with the burial cloth that had been around Jesus' head. The cloth was folded up by itself, separate from the linen (John 20:3-7). Why such details about the linen strips and the burial clothes? The body of Jesus was wrapped with a gummy substance that was comprised of about 100

---

[38] 1) προσκυλίω (Mark 15:56) —aorist active indicative, roll to the face of. 2) ἀποκυλίω (Mk. 16:4) —roll up, roll away. 3) ἀποκυλίω (Luke 24:2) —roll away from 4) αἴρω (Jn. 20:1) —take up + ἐκ from the tomb.

pounds of aromatic spices. These spices cling very strongly to each other and to the body. This makes it difficult to get the grave cloths off. If a thief had stolen the body, he would never have taken the time to remove the linen strips, the burial clothes and the gummy substance, let alone have taken the time to fold the grave clothes properly and placed them inside the tomb! The thief would have taken the entire body and ran away before the Roman guards killed him! The apostle John went inside the tomb too. He saw and believed (John 20:8-9). The grave clothes convinced John that Jesus was raised from the dead. Jesus had returned to life in such a remarkable form that it could simply pass through the strips of linen.

e. Appearances of Jesus. When Jesus appeared to His disciples, He was not a weak person, struggling from the loss of blood, wanting medical treatment like an escape prisoner. No. He was in complete health. There was total restoration. For a person who had been crucified, lost blood and died, the resurrection of Christ from the dead is a fact that cannot be disproved. Neither was Jesus half-dead[39] when He was buried. He was totally dead, and He is totally alive. If He had only been unconscious when He was buried, it would be impossible for Him (humanly speaking) to roll away the stone from inside the tomb and overpower the guards outside the tomb

---

[39] Jesus was dead by the following proofs: The soldiers declared Him dead! They would have suffered severe punishment for not making sure any prisoner was dead before being removed from the cross. (Mark 15:45; John 19:33). The blood and water flowing from His side is a medical indication of physical death. After being taken from the Cross He was prepared for burial and locked in a tomb, eliminating all possibility of His receiving medical attention. If He had not died physically, He would not have been worthy to be a sin offering to God (Matt. 26:12 with Lev. 2:1-16).

(having lost so much blood). The resurrection is by the power of the Almighty (Eph. 1:19-20). Such a total resurrection gave the disciples the authority and the courage to proclaim Him as the Conqueror over death, the Savior of the world, the Power over darkness.

f. Living witnesses. Jesus appeared at least 11 times in different locations to different audiences during His 40 days before His ascension:

Easter:

Morning	Mary Magdalene returned to the tomb. Jesus was revealed to her.	Appearance #1	Mark 16:9-11, John 20:11-18
Morning	Jesus met the women on their way back to the city.	Appearance #2	Matt. 28:8-10; Mark 16:8; Luke 24:9-11
Morning	Peter sees Jesus.	Appearance #3	Luke 24:34
Afternoon	The two disciples see Jesus on their way to Emmaus.	Appearance #4	Mark 16:12-13; Luke 24:13-35
Evening	Jesus appeared to the disciples.	Appearance #5	Mark 16:14; Luke 24:36-49; John 20:19-23

Subsequent appearances:

1. Sunday evening after Easter Day. Jesus appeared to them again, Thomas was present.	Appearance #6	John 20:24-29
2. Jesus showed Himself at the sea of Tiberias.	Appearance #7	John 21:1-24
3. The eleven went into Galilee. Jesus appeared, giving the Great Commission.	Appearance #8	Matt. 28:16-20; Mark 16:14-18
4. More than 500 saw Jesus at once.	Appearance #9	Matt. 28:16; 1 Cor. 15:6
5. James sees Jesus, then by all the apostles.	Appearance #10	Acts 1:3-8; 1 Cor. 15:7
6. The ascension, 40 days after Easter.	Appearance #11	Mark 16:19-20; Luke 24:50-53; Acts 1:9-11

Jesus appeared not just to His followers or to those who believed in Him, but also to His skeptics and those who were doubtful. Testimonies from His own could be dismissed on bias, but one cannot simply dismiss testimonies from the skeptics and doubters who saw Him! These witnesses could be examined during the time of Jesus to determine their validity, and none could be found to provide testimonies to the contrary that He indeed has risen. When Paul wrote 1 Corinthians, he said Christ *"appeared to more than 500 of the brothers at the same time, most of them are still living, though some have fallen asleep."* (1 Cor. 15:6) Christ appeared to Paul, a persecutor of the Church (1 Cor. 15:8).

There is a theory that says the people who saw Him were hallucinating. It is impossible for 500 people to have hallucinated "at the same time" (1 Cor. 15:6). If

Christ was not risen, they could also have produced His body or showed His tomb!

The fact that He was seen by so many time and again proved that His resurrection was a physical resurrection, not a spiritual resurrection. The women touched his feet and held him (Matt. 28:9). He even asked Thomas to touch Him (John 20:27). Christ said He was flesh and bone (Luke 24:39-40). He ate food after His resurrection (Luke 24:41-45). The resurrection was physical. If it had been spiritual only, the witnesses would not have been able to touch Him, nor would He have been able to eat food. In addition, the authorities could have produced His buried body. This would have silenced the rumors of His resurrection.

    g. Changed lives. The resurrection of Jesus Christ transformed timid and fearful fishermen into courageous witnesses. Their changed lives testify to the transforming resurrection and power of Jesus Christ. These disciples would not have proclaimed a lie and then laid down their lives for a lunatic. Jesus is the Son of God, raised from the dead. He is worthy of our worship.

4. Implications of His resurrection

    a. Foundation of our faith. Paul says in 1 Corinthians 15:14-17: *"And if Christ has not been raised, our preaching is useless and so is your faith. More than that, we are then found to be false witnesses about God, for we have testified about God that he raised Christ from the dead. But he did not raise him if in fact the dead are not raised. For if the dead are not raised, then Christ has not been raised either. And if Christ has not been raised, your faith is futile; you are still in your sins."* Romans 4:25: He *"was raised to life for our justification."*

b. Foundation of our hope. 1 Peter 1:3-5: *"Praise be to the God and Father of our Lord Jesus Christ! In his great mercy he has given us new birth into a living hope through the resurrection of Jesus Christ from the dead, and into an inheritance that can never perish, spoil or fade — kept in heaven for you, who through faith are shielded by God's power until the coming of the salvation that is ready to be revealed in the last time."* 1Thess. 4:14: *"We believe that Jesus died and rose again and so we believe that God will bring with Jesus those who have fallen asleep in him."*

c. Proof of Christ's Deity. The resurrection of Christ is the supreme miracle to authenticate His deity. He rose from the dead to live forever. Others may have been raised to life only to die later. Not so for Jesus. He rose and is alive today. Romans 6:9-10: *"For we know that since Christ was raised from the dead, he cannot die again; death no longer has mastery over him. The death he died, he died to sin once for all; but the life he lives, he lives to God."*

d. Guarantee of believers' resurrection. Romans 8:11: *"And if the Spirit of him who raised Jesus from the dead is living in you, he who raised Christ from the dead will also give life to your mortal bodies through his Spirit, who lives in you."*

1 Corinthians 15:20: *"But Christ has indeed been raised from the dead, the firstfruits of those who have fallen asleep."*

Revelation 1:5: *"...and from Jesus Christ, who is the faithful witness, the firstborn from the dead, and the ruler of the kings of the earth. To him who loves us and has freed us from our sins by his blood."*

e. Victory over death. The resurrection of Christ conquered death. 1 Cor. 15:26, 54-56: *"The last enemy to be destroyed is death. ... When the perishable has been clothed with the imperishable, and the mortal with immortality, then the saying that is written will come true: 'Death has been swallowed up in victory.' Where, O death, is your victory? Where, O death, is your sting?"* The sting of death is sin, and the power of sin is the law.

f. Forgiveness of sins. Romans 10:9: *"That if you confess with your mouth, 'Jesus is Lord,' and believe in your heart that God raised him from the dead, you will be saved."* 1 Cor. 15:17-18: *"And if Christ has not been raised, your faith is futile; you are still in your sins. Then those also who have fallen asleep in Christ are lost."*

g. Power for Christian living. The resurrected power of Christ gives us victory over sin, and power for Christian living. Romans 6:10-12: *"The death he died, he died to sin once for all; but the life he lives, he lives to God. In the same way, count yourselves dead to sin but alive to God in Christ Jesus. Therefore do not let sin reign in your mortal body so that you obey its evil desires."* Col. 2:12: *"…having been buried with him in baptism and raised with him through your faith in the power of God, who raised him from the dead."*

Romans 8:11-13: *"And if the Spirit of him who raised Jesus from the dead is living in you, he who raised Christ from the dead will also give life to your mortal bodies through his Spirit, who lives in you. Therefore, brothers, we have an obligation — but it is not to the sinful nature, to live according to it. For if you live according to the sinful nature, you will die; but if by the Spirit you put to death the misdeeds of the body, you will live…"*

Philippians 3:10: *"I want to know Christ and the power of his resurrection…"* Ephesians 1:19: *"…and his incomparably great power for us who believe. That power is like the working of his mighty strength…"*

h. Declaration of His divine Sonship. Romans 1:4: *"...and who through the Spirit of holiness was declared with power to be the Son of God by his resurrection from the dead: Jesus Christ our Lord."*

i. Authentication of His Word. If Christ had not risen according to what He said, we would not be able to trust His Word. All He said came to fruition. Hence, He can be trusted, and everything He said that will take place will be fulfilled.

The Ascension of Christ [40]

1. It marks the end of Christ's self-limitation. Christ limited Himself in the use of His divine attributes during His earthly life and ministry, but the ascension marks the end of His self-limitation.

2. It is the occasion for Christ's exaltation and glorification. Jesus prayed in John 17:5, *"And now, Father, glorify me in your presence with the glory I had with you before the world began."* The ascension accomplished the answer to this prayer. At the ascension, *God highly exalted Him, and bestowed on Him the name which is above every name, that at the name of Jesus every knee should bow, of those who are in heaven, and on earth, and under the earth, and that every tongue should confess that Jesus Christ is Lord, to the glory of God the Father.* (Philippians 2:9-11) At the ascension, the Father *"seated him at his right hand in the heavenly realms, far above all rule and authority, power and dominion, and every title that can be given, not only in the present age but also in the one to come. And God placed all things under his feet and appointed him to be head over everything for the church.* (Ephesians 1:20-22)

---

[40] This section on the ascension of Christ is edited from Kenneth Alan Daughters, "The Theological Significance of the Ascension," The Emmaus Journal, http://www.emmaus.edu/page.aspx?id=40503.

The ascension is the glorious coronation of our King by His Father. He is ruling from heaven, and His rulership will extend to this earth when He returns in judgment to set up His kingdom here on earth. We know He will return to earth to reign because He has begun to rule in heaven.

3. The ascension also demonstrates the Father's acceptance of Christ's earthly work. By the ascension and exaltation of His Son Jesus, God the Father set the seal and crown upon His resurrection, and upon His whole earthly ministry. Christ successfully accomplished what He came to do. He rose to ascend; he ascended to reign. We have assurance that our sins have been forgiven by what the Son has accomplished because the Father has accepted His work.

4. It marks the entrance of resurrected humanity into heaven. Jesus was the first man to enter heaven with a glorified body. He is our forerunner (Hebrews 6:20). His presence there is our guarantee that we, too, will be resurrected and taken to heaven. The ascension of Christ is the guarantee of Christian destiny.

5. It marks the beginning of Christ's new ministry of intercession and advocacy. While on earth He accomplished the provision of salvation to all who would believe. Now He begins a new ministry. As our intercessor He continually mediates for us (Hebrews 7:25). And as our advocate He continually pleads our case before the Father (I John 2:1). When we sin and need familial forgiveness, He is there for us. When we pray to the Father, He forms the bridge.

6. It allowed Christ to send the Holy Spirit to indwell and empower us. The Holy Spirit could only be sent to us after the ascension of Jesus (John 16:7). His ascension makes possible the sending of the Spirit to us.

7. It served as the opportunity for Christ to give us spiritual gifts. *"When he ascended on high, he led captives in his train and gave gifts to men."* (Eph 4:8).

8. It allows the preparation of our future heavenly home. Jesus said, "In my Father's house are many rooms; if it were not so, I would have told you. I am going there to prepare a place for you. And if I go and prepare a place for you, I will come back and take you to be with me that you also may be where I am." (John 14:2-3).

9. It anticipates His return. *"This same Jesus, who has been taken from you into heaven, will come back in the same way you have seen him go into heaven."* (Acts 1:11). What happens at the ascension determines what is to be expected at His second coming. Just as He was taken visibly, bodily, and with clouds, He shall return in like manner.

Applications

1. Salvation is found in no one else except Jesus Christ. There is exclusiveness in the Christian faith. There is only one way to salvation. Not all roads lead to Rome.

2. Christ died and rose again. He has the answer to life and to life after death. I must follow Him instead of someone else.

3. I will seek to share the love of Christ with others everyday.

Questions

1. If Christ is less than God, how would it affect your view of salvation, worship and service?

2. The *New World Translation of the Holy Scriptures*, published by the Watchtower Society translates John 1:1 as, "*... and the Word was a god.*" What is the wrong with this translation?

The Doctrine of the Holy Spirit (Pneumatology)

Objective

To know the Holy Spirit and His work among us, and to stay in step with Him.

The Divinity of the Spirit

The Holy Spirit is fully God. He is not a force or an impersonal power. His deity is proved by the following:

1. His divine attributes

    - Omniscience (1 Cor. 2:10-11)
    - Omnipresence (Psa. 139:7)
    - Omnipotence (Gen. 1:2)
    - Truth (1 John 5:6)

- Holiness (Luke 11:13)
- Life (Rom. 8:2)
- Wisdom (Isa. 40:13)

1. His works

   - He creates (Gen. 1:2; Job 33:4)
   - He superintended the biblical authors in the writing of God's revelation "in order that they might proclaim and set down in an exact and authentic way the message as received from God. This influence guided them even to the extent of their use of words, that they might be kept from all error and omission."[41]
   - Supernatural conception of Christ (Luke 1:35)
   - He convicts men and women of sin (John 16:8)
   - He reveals (Luke 2:26)
   - He imparts spiritual life (John 3:5-6; Titus 3:5)
   - He sanctifies believers (Rom. 15:16; 2 Thess. 2:13)
   - He imparts power (Micah 3:8; Acts 1:8), joy (Rom. 14:17; 1 Thess. 1:6), spiritual gifts (1 Cor. 12:8-11), and peace (Rom. 14:17)
   - He indwells believers (Rom. 8:11; Acts 2:4, 4:31, 6:5, 9:17, 11:24, 13:9, 52)
   - He baptizes believers into the Body of Christ (1 Cor. 12:13)
   - He illumines (1 Cor. 2:10-13)

The Personhood of the Spirit

The Holy Spirit is a Person, not a power. His personhood is proved by the following:

---

[41] René Paché, *The Inspiration and Authority of Scripture* (Chicago, IL: Moody Press, 1969), p. 45.

- He can be grieved (Isa. 63:10; Eph. 4:30)
- He can be spoken against (Matt 12:32; Mark 3:29)
- He spoke (Mark 12:36, 13:11; Acts 1:16, 4:25, 13:2, 21:11, 28:25; Heb. 3:7)
- He teaches (Luke 12:12)
- He counsels (John 14:26)
- He can be lied to (Acts 5:3)
- He witnesses (Acts 5:32)
- He can be resisted (Acts 7:51)
- He encourages (Acts 9:31)
- He sends (Acts 13:4)
- He prevented Paul from preaching in the province of Asia (Acts 16:6)
- He warns (Acts 20:23)
- He appoints (Acts 20:28)
- He loves (Rom. 15:30)
- He lives (2 Tim. 1:14)
- He testifies (John 15:26; Heb. 10:15)
- He has a will (1 Cor. 12:11)
- He prays (Rom. 8:26)
- He guides (John 16:13)
- He comforts (John 14:16-26)
- He knows (1 Cor. 2:10-11; Rom. 8:27)
- He performs miracles (Acts 8:39)

A further proof that the Spirit is a person is the use of the masculine pronoun in John 16:13-14 to refer to the Holy Spirit.[42]

---

[42] The word for Spirit (πνεῦμα) in John 16:13-14 is neuter, but the pronoun used to substitute Spirit is masculine (he).

The Work of the Holy Spirit

1. **He convicts**. According to John 16:8-11, the Holy Spirit convicts the world of:

    i. **Sin**. We must recognize that we are in a state of sin and perdition before we can accept the Savior.

    Note that in John 16:8-9, the word sin is in the singular and not in the plural. The Spirit reveals to us our state of perdition, but not on the grounds that we have committed certain faults or even certain crimes (though, in truth, God in His Word does promise pardon for all sins to everyone who believes. *"Though your sins be as scarlet, they shall be as white as snow."* Isa. 1:18). We are condemned before God not because we are sinners but because, being in a state of sin, we refused to believe in the Savior and accept His pardon (John 3:18)[43]

    ii. **Righteousness.** The Holy Spirit convicts the world of its sin and also convicts the world of Jesus' righteousness.

    iii. **Judgment.** Whenever sin and righteousness meet there must be judgment.

    > Peter's sermon on the day of Pentecost illustrates the manner in which the Holy Spirit seeks to bring conviction to the world.
    > *Of sin:* by drawing the attention of the Jews to their rejection of Jesus and His crucifixion (Acts 2:23).

---

[43] René Paché, *The Person and Work of the Holy Spirit*, p. 57.

Of righteousness: by proving to them Jesus is the Truth, the Messiah and the Son of God, announced by the Holy Word, resurrected and glorified (Acts 2:2, 24, 36).

Of judgment: by speaking to them of the Lord's return, about the great day of judgment which draws near, heralded by amazing signs, and by exhorting them to save themselves from this perverse generation before it is too late (Acts 2:19, 20, 40).[44]

2. **He Regenerates.** When an individual responds positively to conviction, yields to the Spirit's prompting and receives Christ into his/her life, regeneration takes place. Titus 3:5 says, *"He saved us, not because of righteous things we had done, but because of his mercy. He saved us through the washing of rebirth and renewal by the Holy Spirit."* Regeneration is technically God's act of begetting eternal life in the one who believes in Jesus Christ.

3. **He indwells and baptizes.** To express indwelling, Paul not only uses the preposition ἐν, but also the verb οἰκέω, to dwell (Rom. 8:9; 1 Cor. 3:16), though of course, he sometimes uses only the preposition as in 1 Corinthians 6:19.[45]

The indwelling, baptizing and sealing occur simultaneously with regeneration. Not to have the Spirit is the same as not belonging to Christ. Romans 8:9 says, *"And if anyone does not have the Spirit of Christ, he does not*

---

[44] Merrill C. Tenney, *John: The Gospel of Belief* (Grand Rapid, MI: Wm. B. Eerdmans, 1978), p. 236.

[45] Charles Ryrie, *Basic Theology*, p. 355.

belong to Christ." Therefore, having the Spirit characterizes all born again people.

1 Corinthians 12:13: *"For we were all baptized by one Spirit into one body – whether Jews or Greeks, slave or free – and we were all given the one Spirit to drink."* Spirit's baptism places the believer into Christ and the Body of Christ. The believer is united with Him and His Body, the church.

4. **He seals**. Ephesians 1:13 says: *"And you also were included in Christ when you heard the word of truth, the gospel of your salvation. Having believed, you were marked in him with a seal, the promised Holy Spirit."* Sealing occurs at the moment when we believe Christ.

The concept of sealing includes the idea of ownership, authority, responsibility and, above all, security. Sealing assures us of the security of God's promises to us, especially our salvation.

5. **He fills**. The Holy Spirit fills believers. Ephesians 5:18 commands us to be filled with the Holy Spirit.

6. **He gives gifts**. The Holy Spirit gives different gifts to believers. Not every one will have the same gift (Rom. 12:6-8; Eph. 4:11). The gifts are given *"to prepare God's people for works of service, so that the body of Christ may be built up until we all reach unity in the faith and in the knowledge of the Son of God and become mature, attaining to the whole measure of the fullness of Christ."* (Eph. 4:12-13) The gifts are given as He determines (1 Cor. 12:8-11). He is sovereign in distributing gifts. We cannot force the Holy Spirit to give us certain gifts if they are not in accordance with His will.

7. **He produces fruit**. The Holy Spirit produces the fruit (singular) of the Spirit. The fruit of the Spirit *"is love, joy, peace, patience, kindness, goodness, faithfulness, gentleness and self-control. Against such things there is no law."* (Gal. 5:22-23)

Gifts of the Spirit – Many Views....but One Spirit

Today there are many strongly held views regarding the gifts of the Spirit. Many Christians believe that the gifts, such as wisdom, knowledge, faith, healing, miracles, prophecy, discernment, speaking in tongues (whether they are human languages or ecstatic utterances) and interpreting such tongues have not ceased, and that these experiences are normative for believers today. On the other hand, there are Christians who believe that the various gifts are "sign gifts" which ceased with the close of the canon, and consequently there are not normative for believers today.

The various positions are illustrated below:

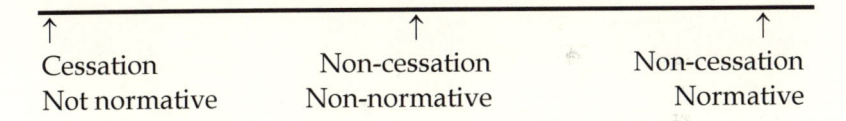

↑	↑	↑
Cessation	Non-cessation	Non-cessation
Not normative	Non-normative	Normative

Cessation, non-normative view says that the various gifts have ceased and, therefore, they are not normative for any believer today.

The non-cessation, normative view says that the various gifts have not ceased, and God *wants* every believer to have the experience of speaking in tongues.

Within the ends of this spectrum are a variety of views where people are hungry for the presence of the Holy Spirit in their lives and find the Scripture advocating their different positions. Taking either the "cessation, non-normative" and the "non-cessation, normative" views to the extreme create situations where God is placed in a box. The radical "cessation, non-normative" people tend to say "God *cannot* do this any more." The radical "non-cessation, normative" people tend to say "God *must* do this today." Both views put God in a servant role rather than that of Master. The former commands God not to do this, while the latter commands God to do it.

The middle biblical view is that of "non-cessation, non-normative." "Non-cessation" means God *can* give the gift to whosoever He desires. He is sovereign, and He can give gifts in accordance with His will. Who are we to command God to do or not to do certain things? "Non-normative" means it is not the normative experience of every believer.

Having said the above, we need to remind ourselves that whatever position we hold to, let us be filled continually with the Spirit (Eph. 5:18), allow the Spirit to control us, produce the fruit in us, help us to love one another, and maintain the unity of the Church to the glory of His Name.

Applications

1. The Holy Spirit always points men and women to Christ. He will glorify Christ (John 16:14). The Spirit will not put the spotlight on Himself, but on Christ instead. Be careful not to exalt the Spirit more than Christ.

2. In areas where Christians differ on the gifts of the Spirit, let us continue to seek ways to unite together and honor and glorify Him. Let us build on areas of agreement, rather than divide over minor areas of disagreement.

3. Let us be sensitive to the promptings of the Spirit. Such sensitivity can only come through an intimacy with Him.

Questions

1. Evaluate the following statements of Christians:

   a. I believe the fullness of the Spirit will guarantee success in ministry.
   b. Every Christian must speak in tongues.

2. What is the purpose of 1 Corinthians 14?

Position Paper on the Charismatic Movement

The following position paper was prepared when I was pastoring The Bible Church in Singapore.

The Bible Church
POSITION ON THE CHARISMATIC MOVEMENT

(This position paper seeks to deal with key issues of the charismatic movement; it does not purport to deal with all aspects of charismatic doctrines and practices.)

INTRODUCTION

The Bible Church is occasionally asked about its position concerning the "charismatic movement." To make its stand clear, two preliminary considerations must be stated. First, The Bible Church is evangelical, and "non-charismatic". Second, the charismatic movement itself is quite diverse, both in doctrine and practice. Some people who consider themselves part of the movement want to be known as evangelicals, others as nonevangelicals. Some are Protestants, others are Roman Catholics and Eastern Orthodox. Therefore, any comprehensive statement about the charismatic movement must make allowances for wide-ranging differences in theological persuasion and church affiliation.

The charismatic movement, as a whole, has had a mixed impact on the Christian community worldwide. In some areas it appears to have fostered spiritual revival. In other circumstances, it seems to have resulted in divisiveness and emotionalism. Not infrequently it has shifted attention away from Scripture to an experience and to certain manifestations linked with that experience.

The Bible Church does not condone the charismatic movement as such, nor, on the other hand, does it condemn the exercise of spiritual gifts when carried out according to the explicit instructions of Scripture (Romans 12:1-10; 1 Corinthians 12-14; Ephesians 4:11-16). Out of a deep desire to be faithful to God's Word, The Bible Church refuses to endorse both the extreme that seeks to impose gifts such as tongues-speaking on every Christian and the extreme that denounces every contemporary instance of their use as carnal or demonic. As a corporate entity, The Bible Church neither practices them nor promotes them. But neither does The Bible Church go beyond Scripture by forbidding or condemning their exercise by individuals or churches whose conscientious understanding of Bible permits their use.

In order to maintain church unity, The Bible Church adheres to the following guidelines: faithfulness to the Word of God; avoidance of any idea of first and second class Christians, which would engender pride, resentment and stubborn self-justification; respect for the authority of official leaders in the church; love for one another. The Bible Church believes that a unity based on experience at the expense of doctrine would be less than the unity envisaged in the Scripture and would be dangerous in the long term.

THEOLOGICAL POSITIONS AND PRACTICES

(I) SCRIPTURE

Position

We believe that "all scripture is given by inspiration of God", by which we understand the whole Bible is inspired in the sense that holy men of God were "moved by the Holy Spirit" to write the very words of Scripture (2 Tim. 3:16; 2 Pet. 1:21).

We believe that divine inspiration extends equally and fully to all parts of the writings – historical, poetical, doctrinal and prophetical – as appeared in the original manuscripts. We believe that the whole Bible in the originals is therefore without error (Acts 1:16, 18:28; 2 Tim. 3:16).

We believe that the Bible is therefore the final, specific, propositional and authoritative revelation of God, His plan and purpose for the world (Rom. 15:4; 1 Cor. 10:11).

We believe that the authoritative revelatory visions and dreams which are the very infallible, inerrant revelation of God ceased at the completion of the Bible (Heb. 1:1-2).

We believe that the Bible is fully sufficient and authoritative for Christian living, and in bringing men and women to Himself through the convicting work of the Holy Spirit (Jn. 16:7-15; Rom. 1:16-17; Rev. 22:18-19).

Practice

No sign and wonder, dream, vision, voice, human statement, impression, and word other than the Word of God should be regarded as the final authority for faith and practice. Any claim of authoritative, inerrant and infallible revelation which purports to stand on the same or above the level of the Scripture must be rejected.

(II) BAPTISM IN/WITH THE HOLY SPIRIT

Position

We believe that the Holy Spirit, the Third Person of the blessed Trinity, though omnipresent through all eternity, took up His abode in the world in a special sense on the day of Pentecost according to the divine promise (Jn. 14:16-17, 16:7-15; Acts 2).

We believe that a believer receives the baptism in/with the Holy Spirit at the point of conversion. This baptism in/with the Holy Spirit incorporates a believer into the Body of Christ as well as endues him with power for the work of the ministry (Rom. 8:9; 1 Cor. 12:13; Luke 24:49; Acts 1:5,8).

We believe that the term "baptism in/with the Holy Spirit" does not refer to subsequent fillings of the Spirit, nor the "second blessing" schema, nor the actualisation of what we have already received in conversion (Rom. 8:9; Eph. 1:13; 1 Cor. 12:13).

We believe that upon conversion, the Holy Spirit indwells the believer and He never takes His departure from the feeblest of the saints, but is ever present to testify of Christ; seeking to occupy believers with Him and not with themselves nor with their experiences (Rom. 5:1-11; Jn. 16:7-15; 1 Cor. 6:19; Eph. 1:13).

We believe that post-conversion experiences of spiritual enrichment are possible. Believers are commanded to be continually filled with the Holy Spirit, and such filling does not give rise to disorderly conduct. Such filling must not be confused with the baptism in/with the Spirit at the time of conversion which is once-for-all and is not repeatable (Eph. 5:18; Luke 1:41, 67; Acts 2:4; 1 Cor. 14:33).

Practice

The Bible Church exhorts all its members to be continually filled with the Spirit according to the command of the Scripture, but discourages any member from teaching, or seeking the "second" baptism of the Holy Spirit as commonly understood by the charismatic movement.

(III) TONGUES

Position

We believe, on the weight of Scriptural evidence that "tongues" in Acts and 1 Corinthians refer to languages (Acts 2:6,8,11; 1 Cor. 14:21, 27).

We believe that speaking in tongues is not a mark of spiritual maturity, nor does possession of this gift elevate that person's spiritual status above others. Spiritual maturity is marked by Christlikeness as the Fruit of the Spirit is produced (Gal. 5:22,23).

We believe that speaking in tongues is not necessarily an evidence of being baptised or filled with the Holy Spirit (Acts 2:4, 10:44-46, 19:6; 1 Cor. 14; Eph. 5:18-21).

We believe that the purposes of the gift of tongues include evangelism and corporate edification, not just personal edification. In evangelism, the tongues is given as a sign to the unbelievers to authenticate God's ability to speak through the speaker a language that is not known to him but understandable to the listener about the mighty acts of God (Acts 2; 1 Cor. 14:21,22).

We believe that the gift of tongues is sovereignly bestowed by God without the need for human intervention such as laying of hands, extreme display of emotionalism, tarrying etc., and such bestowal is not normative for Christians today (1 Cor. 12:10, 28-31).

Practice

Any public exercise of the gift of tongues must be for evangelism or corporate edification, and it must be governed by the biblical limitations, namely, not without discernment of spirits (1 Cor. 12:3; 1 Jn. 4:1-6), not without interpretation (1 Cor. 14:27), one at a time and not more than two or three (1 Cor. 13:1,5). It should be recognised that Christian love (1 Cor. 13:1,5) will prevent us exercising the gift publicly if thereby we cause fellow believers to stumble (1 Cor. 10:32, 14:33).

The Bible Church discourages any person/group from seeking to impart the gift of tongues by any outward manipulations such as the laying on of hands, helping another person to let loose his tongue etc., or to influence other members into accepting their beliefs and practices contrary to those of The Bible Church.

Ecstatic utterances are not to be equated with the biblical gift of tongues. However, some see a scriptural basis for ecstatic utterances (e.g. Rom. 8:26-27). Those who are so convicted should, in the interest of church unity, confine such ecstatic utterances to private and individual practice.

(IV) PROPHECY

Position

We believe that the biblical usage of the term "prophecy" denotes both the foretelling and forthtelling of the Word of God (Mark 7:6; Matt. 11:13, 15:7; 1 Pet. 1:10; Jude 14; 1 Cor. 11:4, 13:9. 14:1, 3, 4, 31, 39).

We believe that the prophet, who foretold as an instrument of divine revelation, to whom the Word of the Lord came, and who therefore spoke the very words of God does not exist today for God's revelation as given in the Bible is complete (Heb. 1:1-2; Jude 3).

We believe that forthtelling is still present and is exercised by preachers who preach the Word of God provided that these do not purport to distort, add to or remove from the Word of God (1 Cor. 14:3,31; Rev. 11:3,10).

Practice

The use of phraseology that claims direct revelation is to be avoided.

(V) HEALING

Position

We believe that all true wholeness, health and healing come from God. We do not therefore regard divine healing as being always "miraculous" (James 5:15).

We believe that suffering, sickness and death are part of man's condition as a result of the Fall. Scripture holds out no blanket promise that every sickness will be healed. We also look forward to the Resurrection, knowing that only then shall we be finally and fully freed from sickness, weakness, pain and mortality (Rom. 8:10, 21-23; Rev. 21:4).

We believe that all of Christ's healings were instantaneous with the exception of Mark 8:22-26. No recuperative period was needed; the afflicted were immediately healed. There were no relapses or misunderstanding about being healed. The delay in healing in Mark 8:22-26 involved minutes only, but the man was totally healed.

We believe that God's normal cod of healing is through the processes He has built into the human body and spirit. Scripture nowhere forbids the use of normal means in the treatment of sickness and disease (1 Tim. 5:23).

We believe that God is able to heal miraculously. The gifts of healing refer to the supernatural intervention of God through a human instrument, to restore health to the body. However, there is no scriptural support for those who go around laying hands on all and sundry, claiming to have the power to heal in the Name of Jesus (Acts 9:34, 14:8-10, 20:9-12; 1 Cor. 12:9,30).

We rejoice with those who have been miraculously healed by God through certain Christian ministries. But we also wish to express caution against giving wrong impressions and causing unnecessary distress through –

(i) making it appear that it is sinful for a Christian to be ill. Not all illness is due to sin and/or Satanic forces. On the contrary, illness can serve the purpose of God (Job; Jn. 9:3; 2 Cor. 2:8,9).

(ii) laying too great a stress and responsibility upon the faith of the individual who is seeking healing (James 5:14-15).

(iii) emphasising physical health more than the spiritual growth and maturity of the person, and

(iv) setting non-medically-trained ministries and gifts of healing in opposition to the work and ministry of doctors and nurses (Matt. 9:12; 1 Tim. 5:23).

Practice

Medical consultation is advised in any illness in addition to individual and corporate prayer for restoration.

If the sick wants the elders of the church to pray for him, he must call the elders (James 5:14). However, prayers for healing are not answered simply because they are prayed in faith but only if they are prayed in the will of God (1 Jn. 5:14). In His sovereign will, God may not always think it best to heal (2 Cor. 12:9; Phil. 2:25-30; 1 Tim. 5:23; 2 Tim. 4:20).

The Bible Church discourages any member from laying hands on any individual claiming to have the power to heal in the Name of Jesus, and it discourages any member from taking a role in healing sessions not in accordance with biblical teaching.

The Doctrine of the Bible (Bibliology)

All religions of the world derived their authority from their sacred books. The Muslims claim their authority from the Koran. The Hindus claim their authority from the *Shruti*[46] (the Vedas), and the *Smriti*[47] such as the popular *Ramayana* ("Rama's way") and *Mahabharata* ("the great story") epics. The Taoists claim their authority from Daodejing. The Confucianists claim their authority from the Five Classics, and the Four Sacred Books (The Analects, The Great Learning, The Doctrine of the Mean, The Works of Mencius). The Buddhists claim their authority from the "three baskets": the *Vinaya Pitaka* (rules for

---

[46] *Shruti* means something which were heard directly from the Gods by the sages. *Shruti* is considered more authoritative than *smriti* because it is obtained directly from God and has no interpretations.

[47] *Smriti* (meaning 'remembered') refers to what was written down and remembered.

monks), the *Sutta Pitaka* (basic teachings of the Buddha), and an organized later commentary known as the *Abhidhamma Pitaka*.[48]

The Bible is the Book *par excellence*. The English word *Bible* is derived from the Greek word which means "roll" or "book" – actually a roll of papyrus (Luke 4:17; Dan. 9:2). The term *scripture* is used in the New Testament of the sacred books of the Old Testament which were regarded as inspired (2 Tim. 3:16; and Rom. 3:2) and also of other parts of the New Testament (2 Pet. 3:16). The phrase, "Word of God," is used in the New Testament of both Old and New Testaments in the original written manuscript (Matt. 15:6; John 10:35; Heb. 4:12).[49]

The Bible comprising of 39 books of the Old Testament and 27 books of the New Testament is God's final revelation.[50] It is the Book *par excellence* because of the following unique features:

1. The Bible is the revelation of God. There are two categories of revelation:

    a. General, indirect, or mediate revelation – God reveals Himself through history, nature, and conscience. Luke researched into historical records in the writing of Luke and Acts (Luke 1:1-4), and John said that he recorded what they had seen with their own eyes (1 John 1:1-4).
    b. Specific, direct revelation refers to communication of truth that cannot be otherwise discovered. Paul received

---

[48] The Three Baskets or *Pitaka* is the Pāli Canon assembled by the first monastic council in Rājagaha a few months after the death of Siddhartha Gautama (480 BC). The Pāli Canon was committed in writing in Sri Lanka towards the end of the first century BC. This is the only canon that has been preserved completely. (Tissa Weerasingha, *The Cross & the Bo Tree* [Taichung, Taiwan: Asia Theological Association, 1989], p. 4.)
[49] Charles Ryrie, *A Survey of Bible Doctrine* (Chicago, IL: Moody Press, 1972), p. 36.
[50] God does not entrust the final revelation to the church, as the Roman Catholic Church claims.

the gospel by revelation from Jesus Christ (Gal. 1:12), and he received the mystery through revelation (Eph. 3:3, Rom. 16:25). John wrote concerning the revelation of Jesus Christ (Rev. 1:1).

The Bible is the revelation of God, having both the general, indirect, mediate revelation, *and* specific, direct revelation. This is illustrated through many of the sacred writers. For example, God revealed *directly* to Moses on how He created the universe (since he was not there to see it), but Moses also recorded God's working through history as he was a participant and a witness of it. God revealed the mysteries of the dreams, and the various prophecies to Daniel, but he also recorded historical facts. David wrote the psalms, but he also prophesized about the Messiah. These writers had both direct and indirect revelations. Whether the facts were revealed to the writer directly, or the facts are already known through historical records, ALL Scripture is revelation from God.

The Bible is NOT a witness to revelation. Those who believe that the Bible is only a witness to revelation believe that the Bible is full of contradictions, and we need to discover the revelation through de-mythologizing the Bible. The Bible is not a witness to the revelation; it is the revelation of God.

"The Bible is not only *a* record of revelation, it is *the* divine record of revelation. Scripture is not simply a revelation from God, it is the only written revelation from him."[51]

2. The Bible is inspired.[52] All Scripture is God-breathed (2 Tim. 3:16). Peter said that, *"men spoke from God as they were*

---

[51] Robert P. Lightner, *Evangelical Theology* (Grand Rapids, MI: Baker Book House, 1986), p. 12.

[52] Sometimes we hear people say that they are "inspired," – this is a modern contemporary use of the term, not the biblical use of the term. The

carried along by the Holy Spirit" (2 Pet 1:21). Inspiration means that the Holy Spirit guided or superintended the authors, without effacing their personalities or dictating to them, so that they recorded without error His message to mankind.[53] The Holy Spirit carried the writers along as they wrote the Scripture. The writers were not stenographers to whom God dictated His message. They were active writers.[54] God uses individual personality, and writing style to record His message without error. The Holy Spirit *influenced* the writers to produce the *inspired* Word. The final *product* is inspired. The *person* and the *process* are not inspired. But God superintended the person who used different processes (such as research) to write the Scripture.

The doctrine of the inspiration of Scripture extends only to the original manuscripts, not to copies of the originals. The original text is no longer available, but the copies, which have minor variations should not affect our belief in the absolute trustworthiness of the Word. Textual criticism has contributed significantly to determining what Scripture actually is by evaluating the variant readings in the manuscript evidence. Pinnock comments that,

> If it were the case that the distance was great between the original text and the present copies, we would have a real difficulty. But the fact of the matter is that textual variants affect not a single item of evangelical belief. The vast majority concern minor aspects which scarcely affect the meaning of the passage in question. The high degree of purity in our present text is a demonstrated fact. Textual corruption is slight and inconsequential.

"inspiration" people received today does not constitute a continual revelation of God.

[53] René Paché, *The Inspiration and Authority of Scripture*, p. 71. Charles Ryrie, *Basic Theology*, p. 71.

[54] Charles Ryrie, *Basic Theology*, p. 71.

There is simply no room for pessimism. Although critics of biblical faith in the past have found it useful in their polemics to allege that the damage was considerable, the charge is quite contrary to fact. A. T. Robertson estimated that hardly one thousandth part of the New Testament was affected. In that case, the problem is removed for Evangelicals when they insist on the distinction between original and copy. A copy which is substantially like the original can function like the original itself.[55]

The inspiration is plenary and verbal. "Plenary because the inspiration is entire and without restriction, that is, it includes all and every Scripture (2 Tim. 3:16); verbal, because it includes every word (1 Cor. 2:13)."[56] So when Paul wrote, *"When you come, bring the cloak that I left with Carpus at Troas, and my scrolls, especially the parchments"*, (2 Tim. 4:13) it is equally inspired! One of my professors said that that was the reason for his keeping his library (his parchments)!

Jesus said that, *"It is easier for heaven and earth to disappear than for the least stroke of a pen to drop out of the Law"* (Luke 16:17, cf. Matt. 5:18). The Scripture is therefore inspired in all and every part of it, even down to seemingly unimportant details.

If there are parts of the Bible that are not inspired, then we will have to determine which is inspired, and which is not.

---

[55] Clark H. Pinnock, *Biblical Revelation* (Chicago, IL: Moody Press, 1971), p. 85. Unfortunately, Clark Pinnock has shifted his theological position from the exclusivity of the gospel, meaning that salvation can only be found in Jesus Christ to an inclusive position, meaning that Jesus is only "one" of the many ways to salvation.

[56] Henry Clarence Thiessen, *Lectures in Systematic Theology* (Grand Rapids, MI: Wm. B. Eerdmans, 1979), p. 65.

If parts of the Bible are not inspired, then we cannot fully trust the Word. If I throw an insect into a bucket of water, and told you that only part of the water is unclean, but part of it is clean, would you dare to drink the water?

Pinnock says,

> More than merely an article of faith, the doctrine of inspiration is fundamental, the epistemological foundation of sacred theology, the basis of every article. Scripture is the *causa media* (mediating instrument) of our knowledge of God, the *principium cognoscendi* (first principle of knowing). The doctrine of Scripture is perennially at the heart of the theological discussion. Our decision about inspiration will affect everything we do. Scripture must be our judge, norm, standard, control, canon. We are authorized to accept no other, and conscience-bound to believe and obey all its declarations.[57]

3. The Bible *is* God's Word. It is important to emphasize that the Bible IS God's Word. Jesus called Scripture "the word of God" (Mark 7:13). It does not merely *contain* God's Word. If we say that the Bible *contains* God's Word, it implies that there are parts of the Bible which are not God's Word. The Bible, in its entirety, IS the Word of God. "In the various expressions the Old Testament declares 3,808 times that it conveys the express words of God."[58]

The Bible does not *become* God's Word when it speaks to you. This view says that the Bible *becomes* God's Word at that existential moment when God speaks to us. It is a very

---

[57] Clark H. Pinnock, *Biblical Revelation*, p. 95.
[58] René Paché, *The Inspiration and Authority of Scripture,* p. 81.

subjective approach to the Scripture. The Bible is God's Word. Period.

4. The Bible is inerrant. Inerrant means "without error." Psalm 19:7 declares that *"the law of the LORD is perfect."* Jesus said that, *"the Scripture cannot be broken."* (John 10:35). James referred to the Scripture as the *perfect law* (James 1:25).

Since God is the ultimate Author of Scripture, and since He cannot lie, His Word therefore does not err.

There are scholars who believed that inerrancy extends only to those that lie outside empirical investigation, but it does not extend to areas where historical control is possible.[59] "Here lies the difficulty: The claim that Scripture does not *err* in those places where it may not be tested is meaningless if it *does* err it those places where it can! The extent to which the verifiable portions of Scripture are fallacious is the degree to which the *whole* of Scripture is discredited. Wherever faith and knowledge are opposed like this, faith suffers. The factual assertions of Scripture are bound up with the theological affirmations (e.g., Mt. 12:41). The theological truth is discredited to the extent that the factual material is erroneous."[60]

Biblical inerrancy does not imply the use of an exact technical vocabulary, conformed to present scientific terminology. The biblical writers used the language of their times. When they set down facts in the realm of science, they expressed themselves without error in regard to fundamental principles, or they used popular expressions. For example, *"the sun rises and the sun sets"* (Ecc. 1:5) is a popular expression even though we know from science that

---

[59] Daniel F. Fuller believed this view in his article, "Warfield's View of Faith and History," *Journal of the Evangelical Theological Society,* 11 (1968):75-83.
[60] Clark H. Pinnock, *Biblical Revelation,* p. 79.

it is due to the rotation of the earth. The Biblical author did not make any error when he said that *"the sun rises and the sun sets."*[61]

5. The Bible is infallible. Inerrant means "does not err." Infallible means "cannot err." Infallibility is a necessary deduction from the doctrine of inspiration. God cannot err, therefore, His Word cannot err.

6. The Bible is Christocentric. The entire Scripture focuses on Christ. He is the center of Scripture. The spotlight is on Jesus Christ. He is the main Subject. The written Word speaks of the Living Word. Jesus said to the Jews that the Scriptures testified about Him (John 5:39). He said further, *"If you believed Moses, you would believe me, for he wrote about me."* (John 5:46) Jesus explained to the two disciples on the road of Emmaus what was said in all the Scriptures concerning Himself, beginning with Moses and all the Prophets (Luke 24:27). Later, He said to the disciples, *"Everything must be fulfilled that is written about me in the Law of Moses, the Prophets and the Psalms."* (Luke 24:44)

7. The Bible is complete. None can add to it or take it away. "Scripture may not be adulterated (by adding to it churchly tradition) nor emasculated (by diminishing it according to the supposed dictates of reason)."[62] Moses was warned, *"Do not add to what I command you and do not subtract from it."* (Deut. 4:2) Agur wrote in Proverbs 30:5-6, *"Every word of God is flawless; he is a shield to those who take refuge in him. Do not add to his words, or he will rebuke you and prove you a liar."* Paul warns, *"Do not go beyond what is written."* (1 Cor. 4:6) Jude says that it was once for all entrusted to the saints (Jude 3). John adds, *"I warn everyone who hears the words of the prophecy of this book: If anyone adds anything to them, God will*

---

[61] René Paché, *The Inspiration and Authority of Scripture,* pp. 124-25.
[62] Clark H. Pinnock, *Biblical Revelation,* p. 96.

add to him the plagues described in this book. And if anyone takes words away from this book of prophecy, God will take away from him his share in the tree of life and in the holy city, which are described in this book." (Rev. 22:18-19)

8. The Bible is unified. There is a unified thread that runs through the Scripture. There is a unity of message and theology even though the Bible was written over a period of sixteen centuries by about forty-five authors from very different backgrounds. Such unity can only be attributed to the divine authorship of Scripture.

John J. Davis says that,

> The beauty and charm of a well composed symphony is enjoyed by everyone whether or not they possess the technical skills to critically analyze it. Symphonic arrangements characteristically exhibit an overall unity, but within that unity there is considerable diversity of movement, tone, and purpose. Such compositions may include great crescendos in contrast to the tender notes of a single melody line. Movements in a minor key and the introduction of dissonant notes, when blended with skill, enhance the impact of the composition.
> The Bible is a theological symphony whose composer is God the Holy Spirit and is no less intricate and diverse in its several parts. Over the centuries, however, some have isolated small segments of that symphony which appear to strike a discord with the whole, and then have called its unity into question.[63]

9. The Bible is authoritative. Since the Bible is the Word of God, it has the exclusive authority over our faith and

---

[63] John J. David, "Unity of the Bible," *Hermeneutics, Inerrancy, and the Bible*, ed. Earl D. Radmacher and Robert D. Preus (Grand Rapids, MI: Zondervan Publishing House, 1984), p. 641.

conduct. It has the exclusive right to command our obedience. Rejection of the Word is an affront to Him.

Lightner gives the following examples,

> On one occasion Christ claimed to be God and the Jews were about to stone him. He defended himself and silenced his critics by appealing to a minute portion of the Old Testament. Two phrases in John 10:34-35 are very important to Christ's teaching on the authority of Scripture. In his question, "Is it not written on your law, 'I said ye are gods'?" Jesus ascribed his quotation from Psalm 82:6 to the law, but the psalms are not in that portion of the Jewish canon known as the law. Our Lord considered all of Scripture to be the law and therefore binding. (One should note also that Jesus based his entire argument on one word in Psalm 82:6, "gods.") The second important phrase is "the scripture cannot be broken." By this Christ meant that it is impossible for the Scripture to be annulled. This passage provides clear and decisive evidence that even those passages concerning matters other than faith in Christ and relational Christian experience do possess absolute authority and therefore inviolability.[64]

10. **The Bible is sufficient.** The Scripture is sufficient to save sinners and sanctify believers. If it were not sufficient, it could not function as *sola scriptura*. There are many today who do not believe that the Bible is sufficient. They say that we need other means such as signs and wonders *in addition* to the Bible, or we need signs and wonders *apart from* the Bible to convince sinners to believe Christ. Such view diminishes the sufficiency of the Scripture. That does not mean that God cannot use signs and wonders. He can, by

---

[64] Robert P. Lightner, *Evangelical Theology*, p. 18.

His grace, perform miraculous signs. But we are careful to affirm the sufficiency of the Scripture.

Pinnock says,

> The sufficiency of Scripture means that everything a believer *needs* to know about salvation and the Christian walk is contained therein. Scripture contains enough truth to lead men to Jesus Christ, and enough to ensure the doctrinal, spiritual and ethical welfare of the people of God (2 Ti 3:15; Lk 24:25-26). Our guides are the noble Bereans who searched the Scriptures daily to see if certain teachings were so (Ac 17:11). The Scripture proved sufficient for Christ and *His* apostles, for they had recourse to no other authority. They thoroughly furnish the man of God for good works (2 Ti 3:17).[65]

If we believe that the Scripture is not *sufficient*, we must consequently believe that the Scripture is *deficient*. If the Scripture is deficient, we would need to make it up by other means such as human authority, or church tradition, or the Apocrypha,[66] and elevate them to the same authority as the Scripture. That would be an affront to the sufficiency of God's Word.

The Bible is sufficient, and it is efficacious in converting sinners, and cleansing the saints through the working of the Spirit. The Scripture is sufficient to equip the man (and woman) of God for every good work (2 Tim. 3:16-17). The Bible is sufficient – "nothing more, nothing less, nothing else."[67] "The Bible alone" means "the Bible only" is the final

---

[65] Clark H. Pinnock, *Biblical Revelation,* p. 96.
[66] The Roman Catholic's Council of Trent (A.D. 1546) pronounced the Apocrypha part of the Canon.
[67] Norman L. Geisler & Ralph MacKenzie, *Roman Catholics and Evangelicals* (Grand Rapids, MI: Baker Books, 1995), p. 178.

authority for our faith.[68] "The truth of the Bible is there by inspiration; the power of the Bible is there by a union with the Spirit."[69]

Let me clarify a few points on the sufficiency of the Scripture before moving on. The sufficiency of the Scripture does not mean that we do not need teachers to teach the Word. Teachers are God's gifts to the church (Eph 4:11). Teachers interpret the Word, and teach their interpretations of the Word, but such interpretations are not authoritative, only the Word is. The sufficiency of the Scripture also does not mean that we do not need to consult the interpretations given to us through commentaries (though that is not our first line of approach to interpretation), but again we must bear in mind that interpretations are not infallible, only the Word is infallible, inerrant, and authoritative. The interpretation of the Scripture according to its grammatical, literary, cultural, historical, geographical contexts is necessary for the comprehension of the meaning of the text, but such interpretation, in as much as we try to be accurate cannot be elevated to become authoritative truth or to replace the Word.

11. The Bible is clear (perspicuous). "The perspicuity of Scripture does not mean that everything in the Bible is perfectly clear, but rather the essential teachings are. Popularly put, in the Bible the main things are the plain things and the plain things are the main things."[70]

12. The Bible is indestructible. Men and women hostile to the Gospel have tried to destroy the Bible over the centuries

---

[68] Ibid. The Roman Catholic's Council of Trent (A.D. 1546) proclaims that the Bible alone is <u>insufficient</u> for faith and conduct.
[69] Clark H. Pinnock, *Biblical Revelation,* p. 102.
[70] Norman L. Geisler & Ralph MacKenzie, *Roman Catholics and Evangelicals,* p. 178.

without success. They can kill the messenger, but they cannot kill the message. They can torture the witness, but they cannot destroy the Word. The Bible is indestructible. The Bible remains the best seller year after year. The French philosopher Voltaire predicted that the Bible would be obsolete within a generation, but it continues to be published in increasing number in more languages than ever before. Jesus said that, *"It is easier for heaven and earth to disappear than for the least stroke of a pen to drop out of the Law."* (Luke 16:17) The Bible, not even the least stroke of a pen would drop out of the Law. Jesus also said, *"Heaven and earth will pass away, but my words will never pass away."* (Matt. 24:35) The Lord said, *"By myself I have sworn, my mouth has uttered in all integrity a word that will not be revoked."* (Isa. 45:23a) The Psalmist said, *"Long ago I learned from your statutes that you established them to last forever."* (Psalm 119:152)

13. The Bible is life-transformational: The Bible has the power to transform lives. *"For the word of God is living and active. Sharper than any double-edged sword, it penetrates even to dividing soul and spirit, joints and marrow; it judges the thoughts and attitudes of the heart"* (Heb 4:12). No human book can claim the power to transform lives. Read the following account of the transformation of a people group by Dr. Pudaite:[71]

> The Hmars are my people. Our Mongolian ancestors came from central China across the lower Himalayas and settled in northeast India. When they fought, they took heads and hung them over the doors of their bamboo huts. The British

---

[71] Rochunga Pudaite, *The Book That Set My People Free* (Wheaton, IL: Tyndale House Publishers, 1982), pp. 10-13. Pudaite later translated the Bible into the Hmar language. At least 95% of the Hmars are Christians now. One of the Hmars became the ambassador in the Indian Embassy in former Yugoslavia, another became the Indian chargé d'affaires in Saudi Arabia

colonialists called the Hmars 'barbaric tribesmen' and said we were almost like animals. When the British tried to take over our territory our warriors fought back. The Hmars took 500 heads in one raid on a tea plantation. General Lord Roberts, the British commander, came after our men with two columns. The British killed a few, but most escaped back into the forest. That's where they were when a Welsh missionary brought the Bible.

Watkin Roberts was a chemist in Wales when a great spiritual revival swept his area. He read Lord's Roberts' account of the pursuit of the Hmar headhunters and felt God wanted him to take the Bible to the Hmars. But when he arrived on our borders, the British agent said to enter our territory was too dangerous. He found some Lushais from a tribe adjoining the Hmars and set to work to translate the Bible in the Lushai language.

One day, missionary Roberts received a gift of five pounds, worth about twenty-five dollars in American currency, from a Christian woman in Hemstead, England. He used this money to print a few hundred copies of the Gospel of John in Lushai. Then he sent Gospels by a British runner to the chief of each village in the tribal area.

The chief in my father's village of Senvon received one of the Gospels. A Lushai tribesman happened to be there and read the book to him. But the Lushai could not satisfactorily explain what it meant to be born again. He suggested that the chief invite the translator, Roberts, to the village.

When Roberts asked the British agent for permission, he was told not to go. "When I go in there, I take along a hundred soldiers for protection," the agent said. "I can't spare a single soldier for you!" When Roberts showed the invitation to the British official, the agent retorted, "That's an invitation to have your head lopped off. They'll make a celebration out of you." But Roberts found an interpreter and went.

The chief received Roberts graciously. But Roberts couldn't seem to help the chief understand the gospel either. After five days he was about ready to leave when his interpreter, who had been listening, took him aside and told him a story. "When two tribes are at war," the interpreter said, "the side that wishes to make peace goes to a mountaintop at sunrise and beats a big war drum three times. If the other side replies before sundown by beating their war drum, that means, "come to the boundary and let's talk it over." The chief who wants to make peace kills an animal and lets the blood of the animal flow along the boundary line. Then he and his enemy place their hands on the slain animal while their spokesmen negotiate. When they reach an understanding, the chief embrace and share in a peace dinner. I believe that is the way you can explain how God makes peace with man," the interpreter told Watkin Roberts.

That evening missionary Roberts explained to the Hmar chief that God so loved the world that He sent His Son to die on the cross – the "boundary" of sin between God and man – to make peace with man. The Bible was a record of God's treaty with man and His invitation for man to come to the boundary and accept God's sacrifice for peace.

The chief and four other Hmars solemnly announced they wished to make peace with the great God of the Bible. Once they had done so, Roberts returned to the British outpost.

> One of those who came and accepted God's peace treaty was my father, Chawnga.
>
> My father became one of the first Hmar preachers. He traveled by foot and canoe all over Hmar country telling the people to come tot the boundary and accept God's sacrifice for the forgiveness of their sins.
>
> My father and other Hmar preachers started churches in almost every Hmar village. Thousands of our people accepted God's peace treaty with great joy. They were so tired of quarreling, fighting, drinking, and living in fear of evil spirits. When they became Christians they began living different lives. God gave them incentive to work harder and to build schools for their children.

Bible Trivia
1. What is the shortest chapter in the Bible? Psalm 117
2. What is the longest chapter in the Bible? Psalm 119
3. Which chapter is in the center of the Bible? Psalm 118 -- There are 594 chapters before Psalm 118, and 594 chapters after that. Add these numbers up and you get 1188.
4. What is the center verse in the Bible? Psalm 118:8 *"It is better to trust in the Lord than to put confidence in man."*

The Canon of the Bible

The Greek word *kanōn* means "rule, principle or standard." Paul used the word in Galatians 6:16. The "canon of the Scripture" refers to the list of books considered by the Church to be authoritatively inspired by God to form the body of truth as a standard of doctrine and living.

God intended for a body of truth to become a standard for faith and conduct. The early Church merely "recognized" that body of truth. Canonization, therefore, refers to the process through which the church "recognized" the body of Scripture to be inspired by God.

The early Church did not "form" the canon. The canonization process took a long time. It was certainly not the result of several meetings. In fact, canonization of the New Testament lasted 300 years.

The primary criterion for canonicity is the inspiration of the books. It is impossible to separate inspiration from canonicity. Inspiration produces canonicity. The inspired books will also provide internal evidences of inspiration. The internal evidences of inspiration are comprehended by the body of believers through the discernment given by God so that the book commends itself to the reader as being different and unique from an ordinary book. God, who has given us His revelation, is also careful to preserve that revelation. God therefore gives discernment to believers to recognize the divine origin of the books. The books are guarded over by His watchful eyes. He loves us enough to reveal Himself to us, He will also love us enough to preserve His Word for later generations.

The second criterion is authorial authority. The author must be a lawgiver, prophet or leader in Israel in the case of the Old Testament, or possessed apostolic authority or apostolic backing (e.g. Peter was the backer of Mark, and Paul of Luke) in the case of the New Testament.

The third criterion is the rule of faith. Nothing can be accepted that varies with accepted Scriptures or that teaches false doctrine.

The fourth criterion would be its immediate acceptance by the original readers. The original readers to whom the books were written recognized the books as inspired and authoritative. This original acceptance continues through the centuries. The Holy Spirit moves among the whole Church to give the books acceptance so that it utilizes the books, both frequently and universally. It is marvelous indeed that all branches of Christianity accept the thirty-nine books of the Old Testament, and twenty-seven books of the New Testament as canonical. God, who worked through the biblical authors through the various centuries to record His final revelation, continues to work through the body of believers to recognize, and utilize the inspired canon.

Combining the above criteria together, Norman Geisler and Ralph MacKenzie say that the true test of canonicity is *propheticity*, that is, God giving His message to a prophet (an accredited spokesperson for God). Therefore only books written by a prophet are inspired and belong in the canon of Scripture. He explains,

> Of course, while God *determined* canonicity by propheticity, the people of God had to *discover* which of these books were prophetic. The evidence supports the thesis that this was done immediately by the people of God to whom the prophet wrote, not centuries later by those who had no access to him nor any way to verify his prophetic credentials. For example, Moses' books were accepted immediately and were stored in a holy place (Deut. 31:26). Likewise, Joshua's books were immediately accepted and preserved along with Moses' Law (Josh. 24:26). Samuel wrote a book and added to it to the collection (1 Sam. 10:25). Daniel already had a copy of his contemporary Jeremiah (Dan. 9:2, 11, 13). Paul encouraged the churches to circulate his inspired

epistles (Col. 4:16). And Peter had a collection of Paul's writings, which he called "Scripture" along with the Old Testament (2 Pet. 3:15-16).

There are a number of ways for the immediate contemporaries to confirm whether someone was a prophet of God. Among these were supernatural confirmation (cf. Exod. 3:1-3; Acts 2:22; 2 Cor. 12:12; Heb. 2:3-4). Sometimes this came in the form of feats of nature and other times in terms of predictive prophecy. Indeed, false prophets were weeded out if their predictions did not come true (Deut. 18:22). Of course, alleged revelations that contradicted previously revealed truths were rejected as well (Deut. 13:1-3).

The evidence that there was a growing canon of books that were accepted immediately by contemporaries who could confirm their prophetic authenticity is that succeeding books cited preceding ones. Moses' writings are cited throughout the Old Testament beginning with his immediate successor, Joshua (Josh. 1:7; 1 Kings 2:3; 2 Kings 14:6; 2 Chron. 17:9; Ezra 6:18; Neh. 13:1; Jer. 8:8; Mal. 4:4). Likewise, later prophets cited earlier ones (e.g. Jer. 26:18; Ezek. 14:14, 20; Dan. 9:2; Jon. 2:2-9; Mic. 4:1-3). In the New Testament Paul cites Luke (1 Tim. 5:18), Peter recognizes Paul's epistles (2 Pet. 3:15-16), and Jude (4-12) cites 2 Peter. Also, the Book of Revelation is filled with images and ideas taken from previous Scripture, especially Daniel (cf. Rev. 13).

In fact, the entire Protestant Old Testament was considered prophetic. Moses, who wrote the first five books, was a prophet (Deut. 18:15). The rest of the Old Testament books were known as "the Prophets" (Matt. 5:17) since these two sections are called "all the Scriptures" (Luke 24:27). The "apostles and [New

Testament] prophets" (Eph. 3:5) composed the entire New Testament. Hence, the whole Bible is a prophetic book, including the final book (cf. Rev. 20:7, 9-10).[72]

The Apocrypha

Normally, when people use the phrase "Apocrypha" they refer to the apocryphal books associated with the Old Testament. There are also hundreds of New Testament Apocryphal books[73], but they have never reached any level of acceptance within any church tradition, in the same way the Old Testament Apocrypha has.

---

[72] Norman L. Geisler & Ralph MacKenzie, *Roman Catholics and Evangelicals*, pp. 166-67.

[73] The New Testament Apocrypha, unlike the Old Testament Apocrypha, does not have a fixed number of books. It is an undefined group of early Christian writings, comprising of a large number of works. Examples of New Testament Apocrypha: Gospel of Thomas, Gospel of Peter, Papyrus Fragments of Unknown Gospels, Jewish Christian Gospels (Gospels of Hebrews, Nazarenes, Ebionites), Gospel of the Egyptians, Secret Gospel of Mark, Gospel of Nicodemus (Acts of Pilate and Descent to Hades), Protevangelium of James, Infancy Gospel of Thomas, History of Joseph, Infancy Gospel of Matthew, Arabic Infancy Gospel, Latin Infancy Gospel, Apocalypse of Peter, Epistle of the Apostles, Questions of Bartholomew, Testament of our Lord, Testament of our Lord in Galilee, Apocryphon of James, Book of Thomas, Sophia of Jesus Christ, Dialogue of the Savior, First Apocalypse of James, Coptic (Gnostic) Apocalypse of Peter, Gospel of Mary, Letter of Peter to Philip (1st part, 2nd part), Pistis Sophia, Books of Jeu, Acts of Andrew, Acts of John, Acts of Paul, Acts of Peter, Acts of Thomas, Acts of Peter and the Twelve Apostles, 3 Corinthians (part of Acts of Paul), Laodiceans, Correspondence of Paul and Seneca, Epistle of Titus, Preaching of Peter, Prayer of the Apostle Paul, Second Apocalypse of James, Pseudo-Clementine literature, Accounts of the Dormition/Assumption of the Virgin , Ascension of Isaiah, Apocalypse of Thomas, Apocalypse of Paul, Coptic (Gnostic) Apocalypse of Paul, 5 Ezra, 6 Ezra, Coptic Apocalypse of Elijah, Apocalypses of the Virgin Mary, Greek Apocalypse of Ezra, Apocalypse of Sedrach, Latin Vision of Ezra, Questions of Ezra, Apocalypses of Daniel, Seventh Vision of Enoch, Teachings of Sylvanus, Odes of Solomon.

This section will use the word Apocrypha to refer to the Old Testament apocryphal books (hidden writings) written between 300 B.C. and A.D. 100.

There is a Protestant Apocrypha, and a Roman Catholic Apocrypha. The Roman Catholic Apocrypha accepts all of the Protestant Apocrypha except 1 and 2 Esdras (called 3 and 4 Esdras by Roman Catholics), and the Prayer of Manasseh:

Protestant Apocrypha	Roman Catholic Apocrypha	Remarks on the Roman Catholic Apocrypha
1. The Wisdom of Solomon (c. 30 B.C.)	Book of Wisdom	**[74]
2. Ecclesiasticus (Sirach) (132 B.C.)	Sirach	**
3. Tobit (c. 200 B.C.)	Tobit	**
4. Judith (c. 150 B.C.)	Judith	**
5. 1 Esdras (c. 150-100 B.C.)	3 Esdras*[75]	Rejected by the Council of Trent
6. 1 Maccabees (c. 110 B.C.)	1 Maccabees	**
7. 2 Maccabees (c. 110-70 B.C.)	2 Maccabees	**
8. Baruch (c. 150-50 B.C.)	Baruch chaps. 1-5	**
9. Letter of Jeremiah (c. 300-100 B.C.)	Baruch chap. 6	**
10. 2 Esdras (c. A.D. 100)	4 Esdras*	Rejected by the Council of Trent
11. Additions to Esther (140-130 B.C.)	Esther 10:4-16:24	Added at the end of the Book of

---

[74] **These seven books (taking Baruch chapters 1-5, and Baruch chapter 6 as one Book) appear in the table of contents of the Roman Catholic Bible. Therefore, the table of contents for the Roman Catholic Old Testament and the Apocrypha shows 46 books.

[75] *These books were rejected by the Council of Trent, but they are included in some of the Orthodox Bible together with 3rd and 4th Maccabees, and Psalm 151.

		Esther
12. Prayer of Azariah (2nd or 1st cent. B.C.)	Daniel 3:24-90 (Song of Three Young Men)	Inserted between Daniel 3:23 and 24.
13. Susanna (2nd or 1st cent. B.C.)	Daniel 13	Added at the end of Daniel 12
14. Bel and the Dragon (c. 100 B.C.)	Daniel 14	Added at the end of Daniel 13
15. Prayer of Manasseh (2nd or 1st cent. B.C.)	Prayer of Manasseh*	Rejected by the Council of Trent

Roman Catholics call the *Apocrypha* the *deuterocanonical* (later or second canon) books. These were "infallibly" accepted into the Bible by the Roman Catholic Church Council of Trent in A.D. 1546, centuries after everyone else had agreed the canon was closed. The Council of Trent also pronounces *anathema* (excommunication from the church) on any who reject them.

The apocryphal books did appear in the Protestant Bibles prior to the Council of Trent, but they were generally placed in a separate section because they were not considered of equal authority. Protestants acknowledge some of the value of the historical background provided by the apocryphal books during the inter-testamental period, but they do not considered them as canonical for the following reasons:

1. They failed the test of canonicity as discussed in the previous section.
2. Jesus and the New Testament writers never quote any of the apocryphal books <u>as divinely authoritative or canonical.</u>
3. The apocryphal books contain historical, and doctrinal errors. The following are some examples:
   a. I Esdras is an ill-arranged collection of much of the material found in the canonical Ezra (Esdras is a Greek form for Ezra), and includes also worthless and

legendary accounts which are not supported by the books of Ezra, Nehemiah and II Chronicles.
b. In Judith, Holofernes is described as being the general of "Nebuchadnezzar who ruled over the Assyrians in the great city of Ninevah" (1:1). Holofernes was actually a Persian general, and, Nebuchadnezzar was king of the Babylonians.
c. 2 Maccabees 12:46 ("Thus he made atonement for the dead that they might be freed from this sin") supports praying for the dead. It is said in Baruch that God hears the prayers of the dead (3:4). Tobit 12:9 and Tobit 14:12 say that almsgiving delivers from death and purges away every sin. Sirach 3:3 says that whoever honors his father atones for sins.

Today there is a trend within some Bible Society movements to include the Old Testament Apocrypha in all the modern "common language" Bibles. This will no doubt cause some confusion and will certainly raise many questions on the Apocrypha.

Illumination

Illumination is the supernatural work of the Holy Spirit given to the reader of the Scripture to comprehend the meaning of the Scripture. Illumination is different from inspiration. Inspiration is the superintendence of the Holy Spirit over the biblical writers so that they recorded His Word without error, but illumination is the enabling of the reader of the Scripture to understand what was written.

God inspired the books

God illumines the reader

The Psalmist said, *"The unfolding of your words gives light; it gives understanding to the simple."* (Psalm 119:130) The Holy Spirit promises to lead the believer into all truth (John 16:13). *"God will make clear to you"* (Phil 3:15) the meaning of His Word as you study His Word. We need to pray that He will open our eyes to see wondrous things in His law (Psalm 119:18), and to give us understanding (Psalm 119:34).

Illumination does not mean that you do not need to spend time in studying the Scripture, or you do not need to prepare your sermons. Illumination comes to you while you are studying, and interpreting the text. The Holy Spirit promises to guide you, and give you understanding in the process of interpreting the text. He clarifies the meaning of the text as we spend time with Him in studying His Word.

Applications

1. The Word will keep you from sin, or else sin will keep you away from the Word.

2. Don't change the Word. Allow the Word to change you instead.

Questions

1. Why do liberal theologians reject the historicity and authenticity of Genesis 1-11?
2. How would a limited inerrancy (i.e. portions of the Bible consist of errors) of the Scripture affect your faith? (In fact, limited inerrancy is also limited errancy.)

The Doctrine of the Trinity

Objective

To know God exists in a triune, and to model our relationship in the community of faith after the trinity and intimacy of the Godhead.

Definition

The word "trinity" is not found in the Bible, but it does not mean it is not a biblical doctrine. Other authors have used the term triunity.

The doctrine of the Trinity states there is only one, true God, but He exists in three distinct, but not separate, Persons who are co-eternal, co-equal and have the same essence in the unity of the Godhead.

The doctrine of the Trinity does not mean we worship three separate Gods. The three Persons within the Godhead are "distinct," but not separate.

The Old Testament Teaching

The Old Testament reveals:

1. The unity of God (Gen. 1:26, Deut 4:35, 6:4, 32:29; Ex. 20:3; Isa. 45:14, 46:9)

2. The plurality of Persons within the Unity

   a. The term used for God (*Elohim*) is in the plural (innumerable references in the Genesis account).
   b. The verbs used for God's actions are in the plural (Gen. 1:26, 11:7).
   b. The pronouns used for God are in the plural (Gen. 1:26, 3:22, 11:7, Isa. 6:8).

3. The distinctions of the Persons within the Unity.

   a. Isaiah 59:20 distinguishes the Redeemer (Jesus Christ) from the Lord ("The Redeemer will come to Zion, to those in Jacob who repent of their sins," declares the Lord.)
   b. The Angel of the Lord (the pre-incarnate Christ) is distinguished from the Lord[76]
   c. Isaiah 48:16, 59:21, 63:9-10 distinguishes the Spirit from the Lord.

---

[76] See Chapter 2

The New Testament Teaching

The New Testament reveals the following similarities of the attributes and works of the three Persons of the Trinity consistent with the Old Testament:

Their identity:

	Father	Son	Holy Spirit
Called God	John 6:27; Rom. 1:7; Gal. 1:1; Phil. 1:2	Isa. 9:6 (cf. Rev 1:8); John 1:1, 14, 18, 20:28, Rom. 9:5; Titus 2:13; Heb. 1:8; 2 Pet. 1:1; 1John 5:20; Col. 1:15-20, 2:9	Acts 5:3-4

Their attributes:

	Father	Son	Holy Spirit
Omnipresent	Psa. 139:7-8; 1 Kings 8:27; Isa. 66:1; Jer. 23:23-24; Acts 17:27-28	Matt. 18:20, 28:20; Acts 17:17	Psa. 139:7-10
Omniscient	Psa. 139, 103:14, 69:5; Matt. 10:29-30; Acts 15:18; Heb. 4:13; 1 John 3:20	Matt. 9:4; John 2:24-25, 6:64, 13:11, 16:30, 21:17; Rev. 2:23	John 14:26, 16:13-15; 1 Cor. 2:10-11
Omnipotent	Gen. 17:1; Job 42:2; Jer. 32:17; Matt. 19:26; Rev 4:8	Matt. 8:25-26; John 5:19; Heb. 1:3; 7:25; Rev. 1:8	Gen. 1:2; Luke 1:35
Eternal	Gen. 21:33; Psa. 90:2, 102:27; Isa. 57:15; 1 Tim. 6:16	Micah 5:1-2; John 1:1, 8:58; Eph. 1:4; Col. 1:17; Jude 25; Rev. 1:8, 21:6, 22:13	Rom. 8:11; Heb. 9:14

121

Their works:

	Father	Son	Holy Spirit
Creation	Gen. 1-2; Isa. 64:8, 44:2-24	John 1:3; Col 1:15-17; Heb 1:10	Job 33:4, 26:13; Psa. 104:30
Indwells	2 Cor. 6:16	Col. 1:27	John 14:17
Sanctifies	1 Thess. 5:23	Heb. 2:11	1 Pet. 1:2
Gives life	Gen. 2:7; 1 John 5:11	John 1:3-4, 5:21; 1 John 5:11	2 Cor. 3:6, 8
Raising Jesus	1 Thess. 1:10	John 2:19, 10:17	Rom. 8:11
Searches the heart	Jer. 17:10	Rev. 2:23	1 Cor. 2:10
Draws men to Himself	John 6:44	John 12:32	John 16:8

The above and many more evidences from the Old and New Testaments prove the existence of three distinct Persons having the same essence and possessing co-equality and co-eternity.

The distinctions among the Godhead are eternal. Christ did not "become" the Son at the incarnation. He *is* the Son from eternity to eternity.

The Heresy of Islam

Islam similarly rejects the doctrine of the Trinity. The Islamic heresy is similar to Monarchianism or Unitarianism which believed in the unity of the Godhead, but rejected the doctrine of the Trinity. Therefore, the Allah of the Koran is **not** the same as God of the Bible. The God of the Bible is a Trinitarian God, but the Allah of the Koran is a Unitarian Being.

Applications

1. There is unity of purpose in the Godhead. No one person in the Godhead will do things contrary to the mind of the Godhead. The community of faith needs to model such unity.

2. There is intimacy within the Godhead. The Father loves the Son. The Son glorifies the Father. The Spirit moves together with God the Father and God the Son. The team is intimate and together. What a model for us today!

Questions

1. Explain Psalm 2:7: *"You are my Son; today I have become your Father."* The KJV states: "Thou *art* my Son; this day have I begotten thee." Does this verse mean God "became" the Father of the Son at a point in time? Or does it imply the Son was created at a certain point in time so He would "become" a Son to the Father?

2. What difference is there in your life and ministry as a believer of the Trinity? Does it matter if you believe this doctrine or not?

Doctrine of Angels (Angelology)

Objective

To know about the existence of both good and evil angels, to appreciate the ministries of the good angels, and to avoid the trappings of the evil angels.

The Origin of Angels[77]

1. Direct creation of God. God created angels (Psa. 148:2-5). Since God created all things, both visible and invisible, He must also have created angels (Col. 1:16; Eph. 6:12; Rom. 8:38). Each angel is a direct creation of God

---

[77] Angels – the word is a transliteration of the Greek *angelos*. The Hebrew word is *malak*. Both words mean messenger.

because they do not procreate (Matt. 22:28-30)[78]. They are innumerable (Heb. 12:22).

2. Time of creation. Angels were created most probably before the creation of the earth because they sang with joy at the creation of the earth (Job 38:7), and Satan, an angelic creature, appeared before the Fall in Genesis 3.

3. The original state. Angels were created good and holy because God cannot create anything evil (Gen. 1:31; 2:3). Satan's original state was also good and holy until he rebelled against God (Eze. 28).

4. Their position. Angels are in a higher position than human beings (Heb. 2:5-7).[79]

The Nature of Angels

1. Angels are spirit beings. Angels are immaterial and incorporeal. They are called "spirits" (Heb. 1:14; Luke 8:2, 11:24, 26). They are invisible (Col. 1:16), but when they appeared to people, they usually took on human form (Gen. 18:2-22, 19:1; Dan. 10:18).

2. Angels have spatial limitations. Angels cannot be omnipresent. They can only be in one place at one time (Dan. 9:21-23, 10:10-14).

3. Angels have limitations in knowledge. Angels are not omniscient. They desire to understand the suffering, the

---

[78] They do not procreate (Matt. 22:28-30), but it does not mean that they are sexless. They are generally referred to in masculine pronouns (Mk. 16:5-6; Luke 24:4).

[79] Believers in Christ are above angels *positionally*, and shall rule over angels with Christ at the resurrection (1 Cor. 6:3).

exaltation of Christ and the salvation offered by Christ (1 Peter 1:11-12).

4. Angels are immortal. Angels do not die (Luke 20:36).

5. Angels can travel with great speed (Dan. 9:21; Eze. 1:14; Rev. 14:6-7).[80]

6. Angels are powerful (Psa. 103:20; 2 Pet. 2:10-11), but not omnipotent. Their power is derived from God, they are under His control, and they act in accordance with His will (Gen. 19:12-16; 2 Sam. 24:14-17; Rev. 6-16). God limits the power of Satan (Job 1:12, 2:6). Angels rolled away the stone at Christ's tomb (Matt. 28:2; Mk. 16:3-4) and unlocked the prison to release Peter (Acts 12:7-11).

7. Angels have personality.

   a. They have intelligence:
      - They desire to learn of our great salvation (1 Pet. 1:12).
      - They communicate with speech (Matt. 28:5).
      - They are aware of our prayers and future events (Luke 1:13-16).
      - They know God's plan for the world (Rev. 10:5-6; 17:1-18).
      - They carry out His tasks (Mk. 13:27; Heb. 1:7, 14).

   b. They have emotions.
      - They sang with joy at the creation of the earth (Job 38:7).

---

[80] Seraphim and cherubim are generally pictured as having wings (Isa. 6:2, 6; Eze. 1:11-14), but we cannot be certain that all angels have wings as pictured by artists.

- They worship God with awe (Isa. 6:3; Rev. 5:11-14).
- They rejoice over the salvation of sinners (Luke 15:10).

   c. They have a will.
- Satan decided to rebel against God (Eze. 28), and a third of the angels joined him in that rebellion (Matt. 25:41; Rev. 12:4).
- They serve the Lord (Heb. 1:7).

The Angelic Appearances

1. The forms of angelic appearances.
   a. Angels appear to people at the direction of God (Luke 1:11-29), either in physical form (Dan. 8:15-17; Matt. 28:1-7) or in dreams (Matt. 1:20) or in visions (Isa. 6:1-8; 2 Kings 6:17; Eze. 1).

   b. Angels appear generally in human form (Gen. 18:1-18, 22, 19:1-8; Mark 16:5; Luke 24:4; Acts 1:10). Some have a youthful appearance (Mk. 26:5). However, angels may also appear to look unusual. Daniel saw *"a man dressed in linen, with a belt of the finest gold around his waist. His body was like chrysolite, his face like lightning, his eyes like flaming torches, his arms and legs like the gleam of burnished bronze, and his voice like the sound of a multitude."* (Dan. 10:5-6) Ezekiel saw the four cherubim, *"...each of them had four faces and four wings. Their legs were straight; their feet were like those of a calf and gleamed like burnished bronze. Under their wings on their four sides they had the hands of a man. All four of them had faces and wings, and their wings touched one another. Each one went straight ahead; they did not turn as they moved. Their faces looked like this: Each of the four had the face of a man, and on the right side each had the face of a lion, and on the left the face of an ox; each also had the face of an eagle. Such were their faces. Their wings were spread out upward; each had two wings, one touching the wing of another creature on either side, and two wings covering its body. Each one went straight ahead. Wherever the spirit would go, they would go, without turning as they went. The appearance of the living creatures was like burning coals of fire or like torches. Fire moved back and forth among the creatures; it was bright, and lightning flashed out of it. The creatures sped back and forth like flashes of lightning."* (Eze. 1:6-14, cf. Rev. 4:6-8)

2. The functions of angelic appearances.
    a. To relay God's message (Gen. 18).
    b. To impart insight and understanding (Dan. 9:21-22).
    c. To answer prayers (Dan. 9; Luke 1:11-17).

Spiritual Condition

Angels fall into two spiritual categories:

Categories	Good angels	Evil angels
Designation	Holy (Mk. 8:38), Elect (1 Tim. 5:21), the angels of God (John 1:51)	Evil spirits (Lk. 8:2, 11:24, 26), "the devil and his angels" (Matt. 25:41), "dragon and his angels" (Rev. 12:7)

All angels were created good and holy in their original state, but Satan rebelled against God (Eze. 28). Once confirmed in their spiritual conditions at the time of obedience (confirmed as good angels) or rebellion (confirmed as evil angels), their spiritual states remain unchangeable and unredeemable. Satan and his angels, therefore, fell decisively with no recourse to redemption and are irrevocably consigned to the lake of fire

(Matt. 25:41, Rev. 20:10). No salvation is ever offered to the fallen angels.

Because of the present existence of both the good and evil angels, there is spiritual warfare and conflict between the good and evil angels (Dan. 10:13, 12:1; Rev. 12:7-9) and between humans and evil angels (Eph. 6:11-18).

Classifications of Angels

1. **Cherubim.** Cherubim seem to be the highest class of angels. They first appeared in Genesis 3:24 and later captured golden images upon the mercy seat (Ex. 25:17-22). They are called "cherubim of glory" (Heb. 9:5). Ezekiel saw the cherubim during his exile in Babylon (Eze. 1:4-18, 10:4, 18-22). Cherubim are associated with God's presence and exaltation of His throne. They do not usually carry revelation from God to humans.

2. **Seraphim.** The Hebrew term *seraphim* means "burning ones." Isaiah saw the seraphim (Isa. 6:2, 3) worshipping God.

3. **Living creatures.** Angels are called living creatures in Revelation 4:6-9.

Classification	Duties
Cherubim	Protection of His holiness (Gen. 3:24; Eze. 10:4, 18-22)
Seraphim	Proclamation of His holiness (Isa. 6:2-3)
Living creatures	Proclamation of His holiness (Rev. 4:8) Purgation of the world (Rev. 6-20)

4. Special names: Michael and Gabriel are the only two angels besides Satan identified by personal names.

a. Michael: The name Michael means, "Who is like God?" He is one of the chief princes assigned to defend Israel (Dan. 10:13, 12:1 cf. Matt. 24:15, 21-22; Jer. 30:7). He is also called the archangel (Jude 9), and he fought against the dragon (Rev. 12:7-9).[81] He seems to be the military leader for God.

b. Gabriel: The name Gabriel means "mighty one of God." He gave insight and understanding to Daniel (Dan. 9:21), announced the birth of John the Baptist to Zechariah (Luke 1:19) and the birth of Jesus to Mary (Luke 1:26). Gabriel, therefore, brings God's messages to man. He is the messenger of God.

Ministries of Good Angels

1. Worshipping God: Angels worship God (Isa. 6; Rev. 4:6-11, 5:8-13), Christ (Heb. 1:6).

2. Carrying out God's orders: Angels obey His Word and do His bidding (Psa. 103:20), bringing news to people (Luke 1:26-33, 2:8-14) and serving the Lord (Heb. 1:7).

3. Delivering God's law to Moses (Gal. 3:19; Acts 7:38, 52-53; Heb. 2:2).

4. Ministering to God's people (Heb. 1:14): They ministered to physical needs (1 Kings 19:5-7).

5. Protecting God's people: The angel shut the mouth of the lion (Dan. 6:20-23). An angelic army protected God's people (2 Kings 6:13-17). The angels will seal the 144,000

---

[81] Michael possibly belongs to the class of cherubim.

witnesses and protect them during the Tribulation (Rev. 7:1-14).

6. Directing people: The angel directed Philip (Acts 8:26) and Cornelius (Acts 10:1-8, 11:13-14).

7. Ministering to Christ: An angel warned Jesus' parents to flee to Egypt (Matt. 2:13-15) and then directed them to return after Herod's death (Matt. 2:19-21). Angels ministered to Christ after His temptation (Matt. 4:11). An angel strengthen Christ at the garden of Gethsemane (Luke 22:43), rolled away the stone at His tomb (Matt. 28:1-2), announced His resurrection (Matt. 28:6; Luke 24:5-8), and, at His second coming, (Acts 1:11) will accompany Him (Matt. 25:31).

8. Gathering His elect at Christ's return (Matt. 24:31).

9. Rescuing people: Angels rescued Lot (Gen. 19:10, 16), protected Daniel's friends in the furnace (Dan. 3:28), and released the apostles (Acts 5:19-20, 12:7-11).

10. Rejoicing over repentant sinners (Luke 15:10).

11. Restraining wickedness: Angels restrained the wickedness of the men of Sodom (Gen. 18:22, 19:1, 10-11), prevented Balaam in cursing Israel (Num. 22:22-35).

12. Restraining the forces of nature: Angels restrained the forces of nature (Rev. 7:2-3, 16:3, 16:8-9).

13. Executing judgment: Angels executed judgment on Egypt (Psa. 78:43, 39; Ex. 12:13, 23). Angels executed judgment on Jerusalem when David sinned against God in numbering the fighting men of Israel (2 Sam. 24:13-16). Angels were sent to destroy Sodom and Gomorrah

(Gen. 19). The angel struck Herod dead (Acts 12:23). They administer the wrath of God upon the earth during the Great Tribulation (Rev. 6ff). One angel will use the scorching heat of the sun to plague the world during the Great Tribulation (Rev. 16:8-9). They will separate the righteous from the wicked (Matt. 13:39).

14. Warring opposing angels: Angels war against opposing angels (Dan. 10:13, 21; Rev. 12:7-8, 13:1-7, 16:13-14). One great angel will lay hold of Satan and bind him for one thousand years at the coming of Christ (Rev. 20:1-3).

15. Attending to the righteous dead (Luke 16:22).

16. Attending the altar of incense (Rev. 8:2-4).

Satan and the Fallen Angels

The origin of Satan and the fallen angels

Satan was a cherub before he fell. The key passage is Ezekiel 28:12-17.[82]

"Son of man, take up a lament concerning the king of Tyre and say to him: 'This is what the Sovereign LORD says: "'You were the model of perfection, full of wisdom and perfect in beauty. You were in Eden, the garden of God; every precious stone adorned you: ruby, topaz and emerald, chrysolite, onyx and jasper, sapphire, turquoise and beryl. Your settings and mountings were

---

[82] Another passage, Isaiah 14:12-15 has traditionally been interpreted as referring to the fall of Satan, but the context speaks of the pride of Babylon. Satan "may" have fallen in like manner, but the text is better interpreted as referring to Babylonian pride. The five "I wills" in Isaiah 14:13—14 expressed the pride of the Babylonian ruler who claimed to be Venus, the morning star, the brightest light in the night sky, and exalted himself above all gods. The Babylonian ruler will die and go to Sheol.

made of gold; on the day you were created they were prepared. You were anointed as a guardian cherub, for so I ordained you. You were on the holy mount of God; you walked among the fiery stones. You were blameless in your ways from the day you were created till wickedness was found in you. Through your widespread trade you were filled with violence, and you sinned. So I drove you in disgrace from the mount of God, and I expelled you, O guardian cherub, from among the fiery stones. Your heart became proud on account of your beauty, and you corrupted your wisdom because of your splendor. So I threw you to the earth; I made a spectacle of you before kings."

The judgment pronounced by Ezekiel on the prince of Tyre (Eze. 28:2) shifted to the king of Tyre[83] (Eze. 28:12) whose descriptions exceed that of the human ruler and point to the supernatural leader, Satan, who is behind the activities of the human ruler. The original conditions of the anointed cherub were described as:

Nature	a. Perfection
	b. Full of wisdom
	c. Perfect in beauty
	d. Adorned with every precious stone
	e. Blameless
Place of dwelling	a. Eden, the garden of God
	b. Holy mount of God
	c. Walk among the fiery stones
Position	a. A guardian cherub

Unfortunately, the anointed cherub sinned against God. His activities were described as:

---

[83] The coastal city-state of Tyre was one of the world's greatest traders during Israel's monarch period. Isaiah calls Tyre " the bestower of crowns, whose merchants are princes, whose traders are renowned in the earth" (Isa. 23:8).

      a. wicked
      b. filled with violence
      c. sinful
      d. prideful
      e. corruption of his wisdom

God judged the guardian cherub:

      a. God drove him in disgrace from the mount of God.
      b. God expelled him from among the fiery stones.
      c. God threw him to the earth (cf. Luke 10:17; Rev. 12:3).[84]
      d. God made a spectacle of him before kings.

The time of Satan's fall

Satan fell sometime between the creation of the heavens and earth and Genesis 3 where he was present to tempt the woman.

The fall of angels with Satan

According to Revelation 12:4, a third of the angelic creation followed Satan in his rebellion and was cast out from heaven.

---

[84] Satan was thrown onto the earth, but he continues to have access to God (Job 1:6, 2:1; Zech. 3:1; Rev. 12:6-10) until he was cast out of heaven permanently in Revelation 12:8. Some believe Satan was cast out of heaven permanently after the resurrection of Christ, according to John 12:31-32, "Now is the time for judgment on this world; now the prince of this world will be driven out. But I, when I am lifted up from the earth, will draw all men to myself." The battle between Michael and Satan in Revelation 12:6-10 occurs during the Tribulation, hence, Satan continues to have access to God but he will be cast out of heaven permanently during the Tribulation.

The Nature of Satan

1. God created him. God created Satan, not in his present corrupt condition, but as one belonging to the class of the cherubim (Eze. 28:14-16).

2. He is a spirit being. The Bible uses personal pronouns to refer to Satan (Eze. 28:14, 16; 2 Cor. 11:14-15; James 4:7).

3. He has the ability to deceive (2 Cor. 11:3), to speak (Luke 4:1-12) and to oppose God (Eze. 28).

The Names of Satan

1. Before the fall, Satan was called:

    a. The guardian cherub (Eze. 28:14).
    b. Some scholars point to Isaiah 14:12 to refer to Satan as the "morning star, son of the dawn" (NASB=*O star of the morning, son of the dawn*; KJV=*O Lucifer, son of the morning*) (Isa. 14:12).

2. After the fall, Satan is now called:

    a. The prince of this world (John 12:31, 16:11).
    b. The ruler of the kingdom of the air (Eph. 2:2).
    c. The god of this age (2 Cor. 4:4).
    d. Satan (Zech. 3:1-2; Rev. 12:9).
    e. The great dragon (Rev. 12:3, 7, 9).
    f. Beelzebub, the prince of demons (Matt. 12:24; Luke 11:15).
    g. The Devil (Luke 4:2, 13; 1 John 3:8; Rev. 12:9).
    h. The ancient serpent (Rev. 12:9).
    i. The evil one (John 17:15; 1 John 5:18).

    j. The angel of the Abyss, whose name in Hebrew is Abaddon, and in Greek, Apollyon (Rev. 9:11).[85]
    k. The tempter (Matt. 4:3; 1 Thess. 3:5).
    l. The accuser (Rev. 12:10).
    m. The deceiver (Rev. 20:3).
    n. The spirit who is now at work in those who are disobedient (Eph. 2:2).
    o. The murderer (John 8:44).
    p. The liar (John 8:44).

The present position of Satan

1. He is the ruler of fallen angels (Matt. 12:24-28, 25:41; Rev. 12:9, 40).
2. He is the ruler of the world system (John 12:31, 16:11).

The dwelling place of demons

1. Some demons are imprisoned in Tartarus for their role in the pre-flood apostasy (2 Pet. 2:4; Gen. 6:16). The word translated "hell" in 2 Peter 2:4 is Tartarus, used only once in the New Testament. These angels were in "prison" (1 Peter 3:19), "kept in darkness, bound with everlasting chains for judgment on the great Day" (Jude 6).

2. Some fallen angels were assigned to Abyss, or the bottomless pit[86] (Rev. 9:1-10, 11:7, 17:8, 20:1-3). Abaddon (Hebrew) or Apollyon (Greek) is king over the angels in the Abyss (Rev. 9:11). Abaddon is the highest-ranking evil angel now confined in the Abyss.

3. The Abyss will be open at the sounding of the fifth trumpet during the Tribulation, and these demons will

---

[85] Both names mean "Destroyer."
[86] Whether Tartarus and Abyss refer to the same place is open to debate.

be released to torment the inhabitants on earth (Rev. 9:1-10).

4. Four fallen angels are bound at the great river Euphrates (Rev. 9:14-16). They will be released to lead 200 million evil spirits to destroy a third of mankind during the Tribulation.

5. Some fallen angels are free to roam the earth. 1 Peter 5:8 says: *"your enemy the devil prowls around like a roaring lion looking for someone to devour."*

6. Those fallen angels who roam on earth are presumably also roaming around the heavenlies (Eph. 6:11-12).

7. Other fallen angels live inside human beings (Mark 7:25-30; Luke 8:26-33, 9:38-43; Acts 19:11-18).

8. One group of demons asked Jesus to send them into the herd of pigs (Matt. 8:30-33; Mark 5:11-16; Luke 8:32-34).

The activities of Satan and the fallen angels

1. Opposing God and tempting men (Gen. 3: 1- 5).

2. Denying God's existence (Psa. 14:1-3), denying Christ (2 Peter 2:1; 1 John 2:22).

3. Deception (1 Tim. 4:1-3; Rev. 20:3, 7-10). Masquerading as an angel of light (2 Cor. 11:13-15).

4. Promoting destructive heresies (2 Peter 2:1) and false religions (1 Tim. 4:1-3).

5. Dominating the nations (Dan. 10:13-21).

6. Warring with good angels (Dan. 10:12-21; Jude 9) and Christians (Eph. 6:10-18).

7. Accusing Christians (Rev. 12:10).

8. Tempting people to sin (Gen. 3:1-3; Acts 5:3; 1 Cor. 7:5; 1 John 2:15-17, 5:19).

9. Blinding the eyes of unbelievers (Acts 26:18; 2 Cor. 4:4).

10. Counterfeiting miracles, signs and wonders (2 Thess. 2:9).

11. Empowering the Anti-Christ (2 Thess. 2:9-11; Rev. 13:1-18, 17:12).

12. Persecuting Israel (Rev. 12:1-9).

13. Leading the world astray (Rev. 12:9).

14. Opposing God's messengers (1 Thess. 2:18).

15. Preventing the Word from taking root (Luke 8:12).

16. Promoting a sinful lifestyle (Eph. 2:1-3).

17. Promoting divisions in the church (2 Cor. 2:10-11).

18. Ruling the present world (2 Cor. 4:4; John 12:31, 14:30, 16:11).

Yet, God uses the fallen angels to accomplish His plan:

   a. 1 Kings 22:19-23, *"Micaiah continued, 'Therefore hear the word of the LORD: I saw the LORD sitting on his throne with all the host of heaven standing around him on his right and on his left. And the LORD said, 'Who will entice Ahab into attacking Ramoth Gilead and going to his death there?' "One suggested this, and another that. Finally, a spirit came forward, stood before the LORD and said, 'I will entice him.' "'By what means?' the LORD asked. "'I will go out and be a lying spirit in the mouths of all his prophets,' he said. "'You will succeed in enticing him,' said the LORD. 'Go and do it' "So now the LORD has put a lying spirit in the mouths of all these prophets of yours. The LORD has decreed disaster for you."* (cf. 2 Chronicles 18:18-22)

b. 1 Samuel 16:16-23, *"Let our lord command his servants here to search for someone who can play the harp. He will play when the evil spirit from God comes upon you, and you will feel better." So Saul said to his attendants, "Find someone who plays well and bring him to me." One of the servants answered, "I have seen a son of Jesse of Bethlehem who knows how to play the harp. He is a brave man and a warrior. He speaks well and is a fine-looking man. And the LORD is with him." Then Saul sent messengers to Jesse and said, "Send me your son David, who is with the sheep." So Jesse took a donkey loaded with bread, a skin of wine and a young goat and sent them with his son David to Saul. David came to Saul and entered his service. Saul liked him very much, and David became one of his armor-bearers. Then Saul sent word to Jesse, saying, "Allow David to remain in my service, for I am pleased with him." Whenever the spirit from God came upon Saul, David would take his harp and play. Then relief would come to Saul; he would feel better, and the evil spirit would leave him."* (cf. 1 Sam 18:10, 19:9)

The final destiny of Satan

Satan will be bound for a thousand years during Christ's reign on earth (Rev. 20:1-3; Isa. 24:21), but he will be set free for a short time at the end of the thousand-year reign to deceive the nations. He will be thrown into the lake of fire eternally (Rev. 20:10).

Applications

1. We acknowledge the position and power of the angels, but they are not to be worshipped (Col. 2:18; Rev. 22:9). There has been a surge in the interest in angels in recent years, but they must never replace Christ.

2. Evil angels can disguise themselves as the angel of light, so we must arm ourselves with Biblical truths to discern the trappings of the evil one. Refuse to rationalize sin. Confess it before God and ask for His forgiveness.

Questions

1. Can Christians be possessed by demons?

2. In the account of Saul's consultation with the witch of Endore in 1 Samuel 28:8-19, do you think a demon impersonated Samuel? Why or why not?

3. Read the following testimony on angelic protection in response to prayers:

> A missionary on furlough told this true story while visiting his home church in Michigan: "While serving at a small field hospital in Africa, every two weeks I traveled by bicycle through the jungle to a nearby city for supplies. This was a journey of two days and required

camping overnight at the halfway point. On one of these journeys, I arrived in the city where I planned to collect money from a bank, purchase medicine and supplies, and then begin my two-day journey back to the field hospital. Upon arrival in the city, I observed two men fighting, one of whom had been seriously injured. I treated him for his injuries and at the same time talked to him about the Lord Jesus Christ.

"I then traveled two days, camping overnight, and arrived home without incident. Two weeks later I repeated my journey. Upon arriving in the city, I was approached by the young man I had treated. He told me that he had known I carried money and medicines. He said, 'Some friends and I followed you into the jungle, knowing you would camp overnight. We planned to kill you and take your money and drugs. But just as we were about to move into your camp, we saw that you were surrounded by 26 armed guards.' At this I laughed and said that I was certainly alone at that jungle campsite. The young man pressed the point, however, and said, 'No sir, I was not the only person to see the guards. My five friends also saw them, and we all counted them. It was because of those guards that we were afraid and left you alone.'"

At this point in the sermon, one of the men in the congregation jumped to his feet and interrupted the missionary and asked if he (the missionary) could tell him the exact day this had happened. The missionary told the congregation the date, and the man who interrupted told him this story: "On the night of your incident in Africa, it was morning here and I was preparing to go play golf. I was about to putt when I felt the urge to pray for you. In fact, the urging of the Lord was so strong, I called men in this church to meet with me here in the sanctuary to pray for you. Would all of those men who met with me on that day stand up?" The men who had met together to pray that day stood up. The missionary wasn't concerned with who they were; he was too busy counting how many men he saw. There were 26.

The Doctrine of the Human Race (Anthropology)

Objective

To understand the doctrine of the human race so as to appreciate the grace of God and our dependence on Him.

The Creation of Man

1. God created man and woman in His own image, in His likeness (Gen. 1:26-27, 5:1, 9:6; 1 Cor. 11:7; James 3:9). What is the image of God?

    a. It is not a physical likeness because God is spirit. He is incorporeal and immaterial.

    b. It is a mental likeness. God is an intelligent Being, and He has endowed human beings with mental capacities. We have the capacity to reason, think and command dominion over the earth.

c. It is a moral likeness. God is a moral Being, and He has endowed us with a moral consciousness. Adam and Eve hid themselves after they had eaten the fruit. Their action shows their moral consciousness. The following make up the moral constitution of man:

   i. **Conscience:** We have a conscience (fallen and darken after the fall [1 Cor. 8:7; 1 Tim. 4:2; Titus 1:15; cf. Heb. 9:14; 10:22]), and he knows a sense of right from wrong in his heart (Acts 23:1, 24:16; Rom. 9:1; 1 Cor. 4:4, 8:7-12, 10:25-29; 2 Cor. 1:12, 4:2, 5:11, 1 Tim. 1:5, 19, 3:9; 2 Tim. 1:3; Heb. 9:9, 10:22, 13:18; 1 Pet. 3:16, 21).

   ii. **Will:** We have a will and the power to choose (Rom. 7:15-25; 1 Tim. 6:9; James 4:4). After the Fall, there was a bondage of the will so that we are rendered incapable of not sinning, and, hence, the Spirit of God must work in us to turn us toward God (John 7:17; Phil. 2:13).

d. It is a social likeness. God has a social nature, and the members of the Godhead maintain an intimate relationship with one another. God has also endowed human beings with the need for communion and companionship. God provided Adam with a companion (Eve) so he would not be alone.

> God has made humans – male and female – in his image, which includes creative freedom and the ability and freedom to make value judgments, such as the following:
>
> Aesthetic: "this is beautiful, that is ugly"
> Cultural: "this is noble, that is vulgar"
> Moral: "this is right, that is wrong"
> Epistemological: "this is true, that is false."
>
> These freedoms are the essence of being creative creatures. God created nature through his Word, wisdom, knowledge and understanding. We, in his image bearers, create culture similarly using language, wisdom, knowledge, and the understanding that God gives. Denial of individual freedom destroys what it means to be human. It stifles our creativity, our ability to give our best to our nation and our world.[87]

2. God created man through a direct, special and immediate act. God created man from the dust of the ground. *"The Lord God formed the man from the dust of the ground and breathed into his nostrils the breath of life, and the man became a living being."* (Gen. 2:7) The Lord formed the woman from the rib taken from the man (Gen. 2:22). The creation is, therefore, direct, special and immediate. We are not evolved or re-incarnated.

3. God created man/woman as a single, unitary living being. The various parts of the body, both material and immaterial, are joined together in a single unitary being (Gen. 2:7; 1 Cor. 12:12). There is unity in diversity.

---

[87] Vishal Mangalwadi, *The Quest for Freedom and Dignity* (Willernie, MN: South Asian Resources, 2001), p. 106.

4. God created the entire human race in Adam (Gen. 46:26; Acts 17:26 Romans 5:15-19; Hebrews 7:10).

5. God created the first man and woman without sin because God cannot create anything or anyone sinful. The first couple had the privilege of unbroken fellowship with God and were without sin until they sinned (Gen. 3).

6. God created male and female; not anything in-between or half-male/half-female (Gen. 1:27; 2:7; Matt. 19:4).

7. God created man/woman with a material body. All of us agree man/ woman has a material or physical body. But some believe the material body is sinful and has to be subjected to asceticism to purge itself of sins. The Bible never considers the physical body itself sinful. It can become an instrument of sin, but it is not sinful by itself. The Greek word translated "body" or "flesh" is *sarx,* and it can refer to tissue (Luke 24:39) or to the whole material part of man/woman (1 Cor. 15:39; Heb. 5:7). In Luke 24:39 and Hebrews 5:7 it is used regarding Jesus' body. If one considers the material body sinful, then Jesus must also have been sinful. That would be heresy! The word *sarx* can also be used to refer to the immaterial part of man/woman that has the disposition toward sin (Rom. 7:18; 1 Cor. 3:3; 2 Cor. 1:12; Gal. 5:17; Col. 2:18; 2 Pet. 2:10; 1 John 2:16). When so used, it is not referring to the physical body itself, but that facet of the immaterial part given over to sin.

Our present existence in the *body,* and a *bodily* future existence reaffirm that we are not mere spiritual fragments of an impersonal god, trapped in "evil" physical bodies, trying to work our way back to our source. God created us as beings *separate* from Himself.[88]

8. God created man/woman with an immaterial nature. Man/woman has a material body as well as an immaterial nature. The immaterial nature is his soul[89] and spirit. God created man and woman as spiritual beings. God *"breathed into his nostrils the breath of life, and the man became a living being."* (Gen. 2:7) We are therefore, as Herbert Benson, the associate professor of medicine at Harvard Medical School, puts it, "wired for God."[90]

There are, however, disagreements among scholars as to whether soul and spirit are the same. Those who believe that soul and spirit are the same say man/woman is, therefore, made of two parts: material and immaterial. Those who believe this are called dichotomists[91]. Those who believe that soul and spirit as different say man/woman is made up of three distinct elements:

---

[88] John Snyder, *Reincarnation vs. Resurrection* (Chicago, IL: Moody Press, 1984), p. 64.

[89] The "soul" is ascribed to the Lord (Isa. 42:1; Heb 10:38). The highest place in religion is ascribed to the soul (Mark 12:30; Luke 1:46; Heb 6:19; James 1:21) (Henry Clarence Thiessen, *Lectures in Systematic Theology*, p. 160.)

[90] Herbert Benson, with Marg Stark, *Timeless Healing* (New York, NY: Simon & Schuster, 1996), pp. 193-213. Benson is still an agnostic.

[91] The supports for the dichotomy view are (1) The terms "soul" and "spirit" seem to be used interchangeably in Gen 41:8 and Ps. 42:6; Matt. 20:28 and 27:50; John 12:27 and 13:21; Heb 12:23 and Rev 6:9. (2) Body and soul (or spirit) are spoken of as constituting the whole of man (Matt 10:28; 1 Cor 5:3; 3 John 2), and to lose the soul is to lose all (Matt 16:26; Mark 8:36f) (3) Jesus did not refer to the "spirit" in His reply to the young man, "Love the Lord your God with all your heart and with all your soul and with all your mind and with all your strength" (Mark 12:30). It seems that He has the material and the immaterial parts of man in view. Incidentally, no one seems to build a case for a five-fold constitution of man from Mark 12:30 (body, heart, soul, mind, strength). (Henry Clarence Thiessen, *Lectures in Systematic Theology*, p. 160.)

body, soul and spirit. Those who believe this are called trichotomists.[92]

In Asian context, we are confronted with non-Christian religions views concerning the soul's origin and the birth of human beings. The various views follow:

Christianity	Buddhism	Hinduism
The human race was immediately created in Adam, and the soul and body are propagated from him by natural generation.[93]	There is no existence or transmigration of the soul.[94]	The soul of the dead is transmigrated into another existence (re-incarnation) when *desire* still exists through the cycle of rebirth (samsāra) due to karma.

---

[92] The supports for the trichotomy view are 1 Thessalonians 5:23, and Hebrews 4:12 where the authors seem to think of body, soul, and spirit as three distinct parts of man's nature.

[93] This is called the Traducian theory. David said that he was sinful from the time his mother conceived him (Psa. 51:5), i.e. he inherited a deprived soul from his mother. We derived our sinful nature by natural generation (Job 14:4, 15:14; Psa. 51:5, 58:3; John 3:6; Eph. 2:3). Christ, however, did not inherit a sinful nature because He was conceived by the Holy Spirit. Other views on the transmission of man's soul are: (1) Creationism: God creates the soul at the time of conception. The problem with this view is that God has ceased from the act of creation, and that He cannot create a sinful soul. A slightly modified view is that God created all human souls perfect and sinless, and allows the soul to enter the body at the time of conception, but the soul becomes defective through the inherited guilt of the body of the parent. (2) Re-incarnation: The soul from the previous existence is re-incarnated into the new form of existence.

[94] Buddhism has a doctrine of Anattā (No-self) says that man is a combination of physical and mental aggregates working together interdependently in a flux of momentary change. The continuity of this psycho-physical phenomenon is bound together by the "kammic" force and is conditioned by "kamma." According to Buddhism, there are three factors necessary for the birth of a human being: the female ovum, the male sperm and "kammic" energy" sent forth by a dying person at the moment of his death, but there is no transmigration of a soul. (Tissa Weerasingha, *The Cross & the Bo Tree*, p. 27.).

9. God created man/woman to be different from animals: Man/woman is different from animals because (a) animals were not made in the image of God, (b) God did not breathe the breath of life into animals, (c) animals cannot provide companionship or satisfy the social needs of man/woman; (d) the soul or spirit in beasts is irrational and mortal, but in man/woman it is rational and immortal (Ecc. 3:21; Rev. 16:3); (e) Paul wrote in 1 Cor. 15:39: *"All flesh is not the same: Men have one kind of flesh, animals have another, birds another and fish another."*

10. Man/woman is a *product* of God's creation, not a *process* in a constant state of flux. According to Buddhist's doctrine of *Anattā* (no self), there is no "I" or "being" in reality, and the so-called "I" or "being" is a combination of physical and mental aggregates, working together interdependently in a flux of momentary change, bound together by the *kammic* force, and conditioned by *kamma*.[95]

11. Man/woman is a product of *God's creation,* not a product of *chance,* or accident, or evolution. Brandon Carter, a well-established astrophysicist and cosmologists from Cambridge University presented a paper in Kraków, Poland in the fall of 1973 in which he mentioned that "all the seemingly arbitrary and unrelated constants in physics have one strange thing in common – these are precisely the values you need if you want to have a universe capable of producing life."[96] This is called the

---

[95] Tissa Weerasingha, *The Cross & the Bo Tree*, pp. 27-28. Buddhism believes that there are five aggregates or *Khandhas: rupata* (shape), *vedana* (feeling), *sahana* (realistic ideation), *sankara* (synthesized formulation), *vijnana* (consciousness and reflection from self).

[96] Patrick Glynn, *God. The Evidence. The Reconciliation of Faith and Reason in a Postsecular World*, p. 22.

"anthropic principle." Carter said that any tinkering with the gravitational constant in relation to electromagnetism would have resulted in a universe with no middling stars like our sun, but only cooler "red" or hotter "blue" ones – incapable of sustaining life's evolution. Any weakening of the nuclear "strong" force would have resulted in a universe consisting of hydrogen and not a single other element. That would mean no oxygen, no water, nothing but hydrogen.[97] The environment, the air we breathe, are all prepared by God for life existence. Life never happened by chance. Life is precious.

God created man and woman. We are special. We are created in His image. We are the crown of His creation. He prepared the environment to sustain life. We are objects of His love, and He came to die for us all. No one should despise another because of color, caste, race, or intellectual capacity. Unfortunately, rejection due to caste still exists, as Vishal Mangalwadi recounts the following story:[98]

> In 1916, Baba Saheb Dr. Bhimaro Ambedkar became the first "untouchable" to receive a Ph.D. in Economics from Columbia University, New York. He returned to serve Maharaja Gaekwad in Baroda who had sponsored his studies. Even as a minister of the princely state, Dr. Ambedkar could not find a room to rent. His caste folk had no spare rooms; those who did, would not rent it to him.
>
> He was the chief in his ministry. Yet, his subordinates would not touch him. The clerks had to bring papers to him

---

[97] Ibid., p. 28.
[98] Vishal Mangalwadi, *The Quest for Freedom & Dignity*, pp. 85-86. Unfortunately Dr. Ambedkar converted to Buddhism and led over 300,000 of his followers into Buddhism too.

for his signature, but instead of giving them to him in his hands they would throw them on his table. Needless to say, he was not "allowed" to go to their tables.

Dr. Ambedkar endured the humiliation. But working in Baroda became impossible after the upper castes managed to get him evicted from the only hotel room that a Parsi proprietor had rented to him. He left Bombay (now Mumbai) and became a professor of Economics at the Sydenham College of Commerce. Two years later he went to England to study law. He earned a Doctor of Science degree at London University, returning to the Bombay High Court in 1924. His merit and fame did not give him dignity. The upper castes became so jealous and irritated by this that they made life extremely difficult for him and ultimately hounded him into the public arena.

Baba Saheb began his public life by leading a campaign to enable his community to use the public well in a suburb of Bombay, where he was then living. On Christmas day 1927, he created a stir by publicly burning a copy of *Manusmruti* – the code of Manu – the most important religious document that the Brahmins use to justify the caste system and untouchability. The same year he was appointed a member of the Legislative Council of the Bombay Presidency. His campaign to enable "untouchables" to worship in a Hindu temple in Nasik made him a national figure. In 1930, the Prime Minister of England invited him to represent the depressed classes in the famous Round Table Conference, where serious discussions regarding India's independence began. By 1933, Mahatma Gandhi had begun to see Dr. Ambedkar as his chief rival for leadership of the lower castes.

Mahatma Gandhi went on his longest "fast unto death" to deny the depressed classes the right to elect their own

> legislators. To save Mahatma Gandhi's life, Baba Saheb surrendered that most significant political tool that the British Prime Minister had given to the lower castes. Yet, the upper castes kept heaping insults and abuses on him. Thus from 1916-35, for two whole decades, Dr. Ambedkar tried to find liberty and dignity for himself and his people through education, employment, political power and socio-legal activism. His experiences led to deeper and greater frustration. So finally, in 1935 he made his revolutionary announcement: "I was born a Hindu, I had no choice. I will not die a Hindu because I do have a choice."

Such discrimination and inhumane treatment upon another human being as recounted above exists not only in India, but all over the world. In China, you can abort a baby girl for as little of US$4.00 when the sex of the child is known. In Africa, there is a common practice of female genital mutilation. Untold millions of innocent have been slaughtered in Asia, Africa, Europe, Australia, America, Latin America, and South America.

The biblical doctrine of humankind gives man and woman dignity. The doctrine should revolutionalized our lives. We are His precious creation. We have a wonderful God.

The Fall of Man & Woman

1. Satan, in the form of the serpent,[99] tempted Adam and Eve in the Garden of Eden (Gen. 3:1-5). He used the following methods *progressively* to lead the woman to sin:

---

[99] Strangely the woman was not surprised at a "talking" snake.

a. *Diluting* God's command (Satan changed the word "command" of Genesis 2:16 to "say" in Genesis 3:1).
   b. *Doubting* God (Did God really say…).
   c. *Denying* God's Word (You will not surely die).

2. The woman fell into Satan's trap:

   a. She followed Satan in *diluting* God's Word. The serpent used the word "say" instead of the word "command," and the woman picked up this word from Satan when she said, "But God did *say*…" (emphasis mine). She began to dilute God's Word without even knowing it!
   b. She *added* to God's Word when she said, "You must not touch it." (Gen. 3:3) God did not say they could not touch it. She added her words to God's Word.
   c. She *placed restrictions* on God's Word. God commanded: "You are free to eat from any tree in the garden" (Gen. 2:16) or "Of every tree of the garden thou mayest freely eat." (KJV) God gave them "freedom" to eat from any tree in the garden. The use of the word "free" is important because it emphasizes God's permission for them to eat "freely." But the woman said unto the serpent: "We may eat of the fruit of the trees of the garden," (Gen. 3:2) without using the word "free" or "freely." A restriction is placed upon their freedom. The next restriction is not touching the fruit. The man and woman had a propensity toward restricting themselves over what God permitted. It all happened very early in the garden!
   d. She *deleted* the word "surely" when she said, "…you will die" (Gen. 3:3). God had commanded: "…you will surely die" (Gen. 2:17).

There is, therefore, a downward spiral beginning with *dilution*, then moving on to *addition* and *restrictions*, and finally *deletion* of God's Word.

3. The man is not exempt from responsibility. Adam could not claim innocence. Genesis 3:6 says Adam "was with her." Adam was near or next to her during the entire conversation between the serpent and his wife, and he did nothing to stop the temptation. Secondly, where was the woman when God gave the command in Genesis 2:16-17? The woman was not created until Genesis 2:22, so, therefore, it was man's responsibility to impart accurately God's truth to the woman whom God gave to him.

4. The woman and the man both sinned against God. Genesis 3:6-7 records, *"When the woman saw that the fruit of the tree was good for food and pleasing to the eye, and also desirable for gaining wisdom, she took some and ate it. She also gave some to her husband, who was with her, and he ate it. Then the eyes of both of them were opened, and they realized they were naked; so they sewed fig leaves together and made coverings for themselves."*

They were given the freedom of choice, but they chose to disobey God's command, and suffer the consequences.

The Immediate Consequences of the Fall

1. The imputation of sin to the human race: God created the human race through Adam. When Adam fell, the entire human race fell with him. All sinned when Adam sinned.[100] We were not represented[101] by Adam, but

---

[100] This is called the "seminal" view.

were actually and organically joined to him. The sin of Adam was imputed to every member of the human race because we are in him (Rom. 5:12-19). All human beings are, therefore, born with a sinful nature, totally deprived.[102]

2. There was a sense of guilt because they made a covering for their actions (Gen. 3:7).

3. There was a loss of fellowship as they hid themselves from God (Gen. 3:8).

4. The blaming game started. Adam blamed the wife, and the wife blamed the serpent (Gen. 3:12-13).

5. They were driven from the garden (Gen. 3:23-24).[103]

The Continuing Consequences of the Fall

1. On the human race:

   a. Transmission of sinful nature: Since God created the entire human race in Adam (Gen. 46:26; Acts 17:26 Romans 5:15-19; Hebrews 7:10), the entire human race fell in Adam. Consequently, the sinful nature is

---

[101] This is called the "representative" view – i.e. Adam represented the entire human race. Because Adam, as our representative sinned, the guilt of his sin was imputed to very member of the human race.

[102] Hinduism does not recognize or deal with the problem of the corruption of human nature. No matter how "positive" a person may think concerning himself/herself, he/she remains a sinner. The power of positive thinking assumes that humans are basically good contradicts the biblical doctrine of the total depravity of the human race.

[103] It was a blessing that they were driven out of the Garden of Eden lest they partake of the tree of life and live on earth forever. It would be hell on earth!

being transmitted from one generation to another generation.

b. Death (Gen. 2:17): The Fall of Adam and Eve brought about spiritual (separation from God) and physical death (Gen. 3:19; Job 14:1-4; Rom. 5:12, 6:23; 1 Cor. 15:21-22, 56; 2 Cor. 5:1-4; 2 Tim. 1:10).

c. The guilt Adam and Eve experienced when they, representing all of mankind, sinned against God continues to plague the human race (John 16:8).

d. Shame of nakedness: Adam and Eve were naked before the Fall, but they were not ashamed. After the Fall, they were not only ashamed before God, they were also ashamed of their nakedness before one another.

e. Mankind's propensity toward blaming others for their own wrongs and sins continues.

f. There will be continued conflict between men and women ("Your desire will be for your husband,[104] and he will rule over you." Gen. 3:16)

Sinful acts of man and woman proceed from the sinful nature of the human heart. There is a key difference between the Christian doctrine of humankind and the Eastern religions where the law of *Karma* determines the next existence. According to Eastern religions, *we are because of what we did*. Our existence today is due to the deeds of the past. But the Bible

---

[104]Some scholars believed that the woman would have a desire to rule over her husband but the husband will rule over her instead. There is therefore a continual conflict over leadership. A phenomenon that is not unusual today.

says that *we do because of who we are.* We do sinful acts because of who we are -- sinners.

Eastern religions:

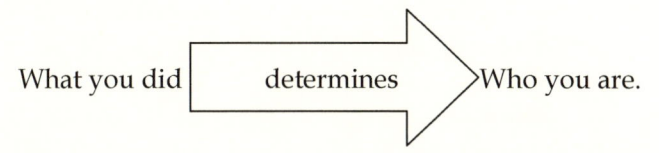

What you did → determines → Who you are.

Christianity:

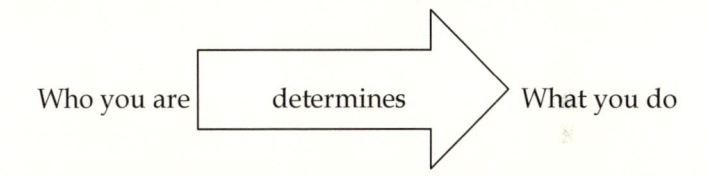

Who you are → determines → What you do

2. On the animal kingdom:

   a. The entire animal kingdom was affected by the Fall (Rom. 8:20).
   b. The animals no longer lived together peacefully (Isa. 65:24).[105]

3. On the ground (Gen. 3:18)

   a. The ground will produce thorns and thistles.[106]

4. On the Serpent (Gen. 3:14):

---

[105]Isaiah 65:24 looks forward to the future time when the animals will live peacefully together again (Isa. 11:6-9; Hos. 2:18). When the Lord sentenced the judgment on the serpent that he was cursed above all the livestock, it presupposes that all the livestock was cursed, but the serpent was cursed above all.

[106]There will be a future restoration of nature to its pristine condition (Isa. 35).

- a. The serpent is cursed above all the livestock and all the wild animals.
- b. The serpent will crawl on his belly all the days of his life.
- c. The serpent will eat dust all the days of his life (cf. Isa. 65:25).

5. On the woman:

- a. Childbirth would be painful (Gen. 3:16).
- b. Ruled by men (Gen. 3:16 cf. 1 Cor. 11:3, 14:34; Eph. 5:24-25; Titus 2:3-5; 1 Peter 3:1, 5-6).[107]

6. On the man:

- a. Work would become toilsome labor (Gen. 3:19).[108] Adam was placed in a garden where all his needs were supplied. After the Fall, Adam was faced with having to supply food for himself and his family. The cost of disobedience is always greater than the cost of obedience.
- b. Man's physical body shall return to dust upon death (Gen. 3:19).[109]

---

[107]The rulership does not give license to man to treat his wife as a doormat. The husband is to exercise loving leadership (Eph. 5:22-33) under the control of the Spirit and in submission to Christ (Eph. 5:18-21).

[108]The curse on the man in Genesis 3:19 extends to the woman too.

[109]Again, the curse extends to the woman too because the woman also returns to dust upon death.

Dukkha and Moksha
(Suffering and Salvation)

Buddhism believes that life' suffering (*dukkha*) is caused by craving (*tanhā*) for existence and non-existence.[110] Mankind basic problem is therefore craving which produces suffering. The solution of this problem is the elimination of craving through the Eightfold Path.[111]

If the cause of suffering is craving, and the cure of suffering is the elimination of craving, then one is inevitably drawn into a vicious cycle because there is a craving to eliminate the craving. The craving to eliminate craving produces suffering, and there is no way out of that bondage!

Buddhism makes all craving/desire bad in the sense that it produces suffering. There are certainly sinful cravings or sinful desires (Prov. 13:2, 21:10; Eph. 2:3; 1 John 2:16), but there are cravings or desires which are wholesome and good, such as craving for pure spiritual milk so that we may grow up in Him (1 Pet. 2:2). The Scripture says that it is good to desire Him (Psa. 73:25; Isa. 26:8), and to do His will (Psa. 40:8). Paul desired that the Israelites may be saved (Rom. 10:1), and he desired to depart from this world to be with Christ (Phil. 1:23).

Christianity believes that the suffering in the world was *originally* caused by the Fall of mankind because of their disobedience to God. The basic problem is sin (*dosa*), not craving (*tanhā*). The Christian Gospel promises that there is

---

[110] This is Buddhism's first and second noble truths. The first noble truth states the existence of suffering, and the second noble truth states the cause of suffering – the craving for existence and non-existence.

[111] This is Buddhism's third and fourth noble truths. The third states the elimination of suffering through the elimination of craving. The fourth noble truth states that the elimination of craving can be achieved by following the Eightfold Path.

> deliverance from *dukkha* ultimately because Christ dealt with the fundamental problem of *dosa* (sin). It is not enough for me to walk the middle way. My self-effort will prove futile because of my sinful nature. My need is for a Savior who is the Way, who will forgive my sins, check my propensity to sin now, and finally remove sin altogether at the end of time so that suffering which *exists* now will be made *extinct* in the future. "From *dukkha* cause by *dosa*, I have come to experience *moksa* (salvation)."[112]

The future of the human race

1. Death – Due to the fall of Adam, all die. Hebrews 9:27 says that "*man is destined to die once, and after that to face judgment.*" We are not reincarnated after death. We are to die *once*, not die again and again. The word *once* means *once for all time*, not *once per lifetime* as Eastern philosophies advocate. We die *once for all time*. This meaning is supported by the context where it is mentioned, "*Christ was sacrificed once to take away the sins of many people; and he will appear a second time, not to bear sin, but to bring salvation to those who are waiting for him.*" (Heb. 9:28) Christ died only *once*, i.e. *once for all time*. Therefore we will die only *once*. Paul expected to die once so that he could immediately be with Jesus (Phil. 1:23). He was not looking forward to being *recycled*.
2. Resurrection – There will be the resurrection of the bodies at the second coming of Christ.
3. Judgment – There will judgments for believers and unbelievers. The judgment for believers is called the Bēma judgment (1 Cor. 3:11-15; 2 Cor. 5:10). The judgment for unbelievers is called the Great White Throne judgment (Rev. 20:11-13).

---

[112] Tissa Weerasingha, *The Cross & the Bo Tree,* p. 21.

4. Eternal destinies – The destiny of the unbelievers will be the lake of fire (Rev. 20:14-15; 21:8). Believers will reign with Christ in the new heaven and new earth (Rev. 21, 22).

The Law of *Karma* and the Destiny of Humankind

God determines the destiny of humankind. The destiny is already revealed in the Scripture -- The unbelievers will be confined to the lake of fire, but the believers in Christ will reign with Him in the new heaven and new earth. Our destiny is not determined by the law of *karma*.

The power of the law of *karma* is CONTINUATION and the direction is determined by the sower. The control of one's destiny is NOT in one's hand either. What is supreme is the law of *karma*. Everyone is SUBJECT to it. As Christian I submit to the sovereignty of Christ while the Buddhist or the Hindu submits to the sovereignty of the law of *karma*.[113]

But herein lies the difference. My submission to Christ brings liberty. Whereas the submission to the law of *karma*, a self-effort to liberate oneself brings the vicious cycle of bondage, futility in its struggle against what plague the human heart, and ultimately brings despair and hopelessness.

Applications

1. Man is corrupt in His nature, apart from his redemption in Christ. Only Christ can transform a person. Education, economics and political systems cannot transform a person.

---

[113] Ibid., p. 37

2. I must seek opportunities to share Christ with others because mankind, apart from Christ, is destined to damnation. This is the reality of hell. We must to be in the business of depopulating hell and populating heaven!

Questions

1. How has the depravity of men manifested itself in human cruelty among us?

2. If God created man in His own image, how should we treat one another, especially poor children, street kids, prisoners, prostitutes, etc?

The Doctrine of Salvation (Soteriology)

Objective

To understand and appreciate the greatness of our salvation, and to propel us to share the Good News with the world.

Total Depravity

All fell when Adam fell. As a result, every human being inherited a sinful nature, totally corrupt in his being (Rom. 1:18-3:20, 8:10) and possessing a propensity toward evil and an aversion to God (Rom. 7:18). Man and woman are incapable of conforming to the law of God (Rom. 8:7-10) by his own volition, apart from the grace of God, the cross of Christ and the work of the Holy Spirit in regenerating and empowering him to do so.[114] He/she is deprived in his/her mind (Rom. 1:28, 8:6; Eph. 4:18), conscience (1 Tim. 4:2), will (Rom. 1:28) and heart (Eph. 4:18). We are objects of His wrath (Eph. 2:3).

Categories of sin[115]

There are three categories of sin. Charles Ryrie offers the following chart:[116]

Aspect	Scripture	Transmission	Principal Consequence	Remedy
Inherited sin	Ephesians 2:3	Generation to generation	Spiritual death	Redemption and the gift of the Holy Spirit

---

[114]Total depravity does not mean we are void of any good human qualities or we are incapable of doing any good in the sight of men, but such good works are considered filthy rags by God (Isa. 64:6).

[115]Frank Whaling, *An Approach to Dialogue with Hinduism*, p. 61: "Sin has no great place in Hindu theology because the Hindu does not allow that sin presses hard either upon the life of man, or upon the life of God. Hogg summarizes the first view very neatly, "If MY sin is really to find me out, I must perceive that it is MY sin and how horribly sinful it is. But according to the *karma*-transmigration concept the sin that is finding me out is always the sin the nature of which I have no knowledge because it was committed by me in an unremembered previous incarnations. Such an experience is no moral searching of the conscience." And if sin is not a burden to the conscience of man, neither, in Hinduism is it a great burden to the tranquility of God. Hinduism has the idea of a gracious God. But this grace is not costly. It is God's ordinary attitude towards man. Even when He is gracious, God stays outside the problems of human life, and the sin of man does not press hard upon the grace of God or upon the life of God. In contrast, the grace of Jesus Christ is a costly grace. Christ agonized for the predicament of man; He wept for the disobedience of man; He suffered for the selfishness of man; and in the end, He died for the sin of man. The emblems of His grace are some nails and some pieces of wood shaped in the form of a cross."

[116]Charles Ryrie, *Basic Theology*, p. 229.

Imputed sin	Romans 5:12	Direct from Adam to me	Physical death	Imputed righteousness
Personal sin	Romans 3:23; 1 John 1:9	None	Loss of fellowship	Forgiveness

Penalty of sin

Penalty is that pain or loss which is directly inflicted by the lawgiver in vindication of his justice, which has been outraged by the violation of law.[117] The penalty of sin is death:

1. Physical death (Gen. 2:7, 3:19; Num. 16:29, 27:3; Psa. 90:7-11; Isa. 38:17-18; Rom. 5:12-17, 8:3, 10-11).

2. Spiritual death, i.e. separation from God (Gen. 2:7; Rom. 5:21, 6:23; Eph. 2:1, 5).

3. Eternal death, i.e. eternal separation from God (Matt. 10:28, 25:41; 2 Thess. 1:9; Heb. 10:31; Rev. 20:14-15).

Power of sin

Because of the inherited sinful nature that renders us totally depraved, we are subjected to the control of the sinful nature and the evil one (2 Tim. 2:16). The power of sin reigns in us. We are slaves to sin (Rom. 6:16-23). The conflict between the good and the evil continues to plague us after we believed in Christ (Rom. 6-8), but practical victory[118] is assured when we allow Christ to control us.

---

[117]Henry Clarence Thiessen, *Lectures in Systematic Theology*, p. 194.
[118]Positionally, we are victorious, but practically we may still live defeated lives if we continue to let the flesh reign over us.

Presence of sin

Sin is ever present in life because fallen human beings live in a fallen world under the delegated control of the prince of darkness (Eph. 6:12). The presence of sin will only be removed at the end of time (Dan. 9:24; Rev. 21-22).

Death of Christ

1. The death of Christ is *vicarious* or substitutionary. Christ did not die for His own sins, but for the sins of others (Isa. 53:5-12; Mark 10:45; John 8:46, 10:11, 15:13; Rom. 5:8, 8:32; 1 Cor. 5:7, 15:3; 2 Cor. 5:21; Heb. 2:9, 4:15; 1 Pet. 2:22-24, 3:18).[119]

2. The death of Christ *satisfied* the justice and the law of God. God cannot clear the guilty apart from the satisfaction of the demands of justice (Ex. 34:7; Num. 14:18). The penalty of sin had to be paid in order to secure the release. Christ's death satisfied the demand

---

[119]The doctrine of *karma* says that one is to bear the consequences of his own actions, but the death of Christ is vicarious, on behalf of sinful humanity. The punishment falls on Christ. He paid the penalty. His death is not the result of His sins. He is the sinless One who died for the sinful. E. Ahmad-Shah notes that, "Mother takes upon herself all the pains and suffering of her new-born babe. Friends suffers for friend, and sometimes even for an enemy. Gandhiji bore the transgression of law by others on himself several times by fast unto death. The law of transference of *karma*, supported both by Samkara and Ramanuja (Vedanta Sutras 4:1, 16, 17, 18), invalidates the strict application of the law of *karma*. Therefore we reiterate that the Christian doctrine of vicarious suffering and death of Jesus Christ is in consonant with moral law. God could have atoned sins by a decree. But he fulfils his holy love and justice by taking upon himself the sins of man in his incarnation in Jesus Christ. Moral law is not evaded but honoured . Sacrificial death of Christ was an execution of law, vindicating God's righteousness and at the same time redeeming man and restoring him to the lost communion with God." (E. Ahmad-Shah, *Theology – Christian and Hindu*, pp. 50-51.)

of the law. God is, therefore, able to justify sinners (Rom. 3:25-26).

3. The death of Christ *atoned* for the sins of the world. To "atone" means to "cover over" so as not to be seen. Christ's death covered over the sins of the world just as the blood of the sacrificial lamb atoned for the sins of sinners (Lev. 4:13-20, 6:2-7; Heb. 2:17).

4. The death of Christ *propitiated* the wrath of God (Rom. 3:25; 1 John 2:2, 4:10). God's justice and the law were satisfied and sins atoned for, allowing the wrath of God to turn away. Christ's death appeased God's wrath. His death is a propitiation of the wrath of God because He became an expiation[120] for our sins.

5. The death of Christ *reconciled* sinners to God[121] (Rom. 5:10; 2 Cor. 5:18-19; Eph. 2:16). It is no longer a lost world, but a reconciled world. This does not mean every body will be saved, but it means the world is savable.

6. The death of Christ paid the *ransom* to God (not to Satan) in order to set the prisoner free (Matt. 20:28; Mark 10:45). Christ redeemed sinners from the penalty of sin (Luke 1:68, 2:38; Heb. 9:12; Rom. 7:4; Gal. 3:13), the power of sin (Rom. 6:2, 22; Titus 2:14; 1 Pet. 1:18-19) and the clutches of Satan (2 Tim. 2:26).

7. The death of Christ is not limited only to the elect. He took away the sins of the whole world (John 1:29; 1 Tim. 2:6; Titus 2:11; Heb. 2:9; 1 John 2:2). The atonement is

---

[120]Expiation is the reparation for a wrong.
[121]Man/woman is reconciled to God. God does not need to be reconciled to us, but we need to be reconciled to God. Man/woman is the object of reconciliation.

unlimited — available for all, but effective only to those who believe.

Thiessen summarizes the death of Christ with the following words:

> His death secured for all men a delay in the execution of the sentence against sin, space for repentance and the common blessings of life which have been forfeited by transgression; it removed from the mind of God every obstacle to the pardon of the penitent and restoration of the sinner, except his willful opposition to God and rejection of him; it procured for the unbeliever the powerful incentives to repentance presented in the cross, by means of the preaching of God's servants, and through the work of the Holy Spirit; it provided salvation for those who do not willfully and personally sin (i.e., those who die in infancy or those who have never been mentally responsible) and assured its application to them; and it makes possible the final restoration of creation itself.[122]

The Death of Jesus Christ and the Doctrine of *Ahimsa*[123]

Atonement through blood raises a serious difficulty for those who follow the path of *ahimsa* (non-injury). No one shall injure anyone, much less shed blood. The doctrine of *ahimsa* goes against the killing of life. To this our answer is:

(a) The lost of life of man requires another life to restore him to his normal life. The blood transfusion operation on a sinking (dying) life is a telling testimony for saving life.

---

[122] Henry Clarence Thiessen, *Lectures in Systematic Theology*, pp. 241-42.
[123] E. Ahmad-Shah, *Theology – Christian and Hindu*, p. 49.

(b) Sacrifice of animals for propitiation of gods is enjoined in many religions and cultures of nations. Vedic injunctions for different types of sacrifices (including animal sacrifices) for obtaining desired objects of life are before us.
(c) There are records of suffering death of mythological gods for man. Taammuz of the Chaldeans, Osiris of the Egyptians, Adonis of Greeks, Balder of the Scandinavians, are reported to have sacrificed themselves to save man. In one of the Brahmanas it is recorded: "Prajapati offered himself as a sacrifice for gods and sages."
(d) Rig Veda 10th Mandal (Chapter) and 90th hymn speaks of Prajapati (Father of mankind, that is, God) sacrificing himself for bringing himself into life different castes of men.
(e) The biblical statement clearly says: "It is the blood *that* maketh an atonement for the soul." (Lev. 17:11) The life of all flesh, is the blood thereof.

Election

Christians are divided over the issue of election or predestination. There are two opposing main views:

1. God's sovereign election of some to salvation and others to damnation was *not* based on foreknowledge (Acts 13:48; Eph. 1:5, 11; 1 Thess. 1:4). The major objection to this view is that election equals fatalism.

2. God's sovereign election of some to salvation and others to damnation was based on foreknowledge. God's election is a sovereign act of God, whereby, He graciously and lovingly chooses for salvation in Christ, before the foundation of the world, all whom He knew would accept Him (Rom. 8:29-30; Eph. 1:4-5, 11; 1 Peter 1:1-2). God's election is not an arbitrary act, whereby,

169

He chooses some to salvation while leaving the rest to perish.

Whichever view you considers more biblical, we must all acknowledge that the finite mind is incapable of comprehending the infinite mysteries of God (Rom. 11:33).

The role of the Holy Spirit

The Holy Spirit works in the heart of the unbeliever concerning guilt, in regard to sin and righteousness and judgment (John 16:8 cf. 6:44), and causes him/her to turn to God. No one by his/her own volition seeks after God because man/woman is dead in his/her transgressions and sins (Eph. 2:1). Man/woman, when so moved by the Holy Spirit to believe in Him, will exercise his/her freedom of choice to trust in Him. That is irresistible grace.

What is Salvation?

Salvation is saving from eternal death and endowing a person with everlasting life (Rom. 5:9; Heb. 7:25).[124] There is much more to be said concerning the richness and the greatness of our salvation later, but we need to clarify what salvation is not:

1. Salvation is not *moksha*. "*Moksha* is the final liberation from *avagavana* (cyclic existence of births and deaths). It is release from this life and many other lives, through which a soul (*atman*) migrates in accordance with the law of *karma* (action)."[125]
2. Salvation is not the merging of oneself into the Brahman, and thereby losses oneself into the One.

---

[124]Charles C. Ryrie, *Basic Theology*. p. 279.
[125]E. Ahmad-Shah, *Theology – Christian and Hindu*, p. 128.

3. Salvation is not Nirvana, the state of the extinction of desire, or a state of nothingness.

Three Aspects of Salvation

There are three aspects of salvation summarized in Romans 5:1-2, *"Therefore, since we have been justified through faith, we have peace with God through our Lord Jesus Christ, through whom we have gained access by faith into this grace in which we now stand. And we rejoice in the hope of the glory of God."*

1. Positional salvation: Positional salvation says that once a person believes Christ as his personal Savior, he is justified, and saved from eternal condemnation. There is peace with God. *We have been justified through faith, we have peace with God through our Lord Jesus Christ.*
2. Progressive salvation is daily sanctification of our lives unto God in His grace. We are justified through faith by His grace, and we continue to live in this grace. *We have gained access by faith into this grace in which we now stand.* We stand in this grace. Unfortunately, there are many who are saved by grace, but live by sweat. The Christian life begins with the grace of God and continues in that grace.
3. Prospective salvation is glorification when we shall be in the presence of God in heaven upon death. *We rejoice in the hope of the glory of God.* Upon death, the believer in Christ entered into the presence of God. Paul says that when he is away from the body, he is at home with the Lord (2 Cor. 5:8). Jesus promised the robber, *"today you will be with me in paradise."* (Luke 23:43)

Praying for the Dead?

A believer in Christ enters into the presence of God immediately after death (2 Cor. 5:8; Luke 23:43). Those who do not believe in Christ, without the righteousness of Christ imputed to them, will be confined in hell until the second coming of Christ when they will be judged, and then thrown into the lake of fire (Rev. 20:14-15). If the person does not believe Christ as his/her Savior while on earth, the Bible is unequivocally clear that there is no more second chance of salvation upon death. The sharing of the Gospel of Jesus Christ is more urgent than ever.

There is no need to pray for the departed unsaved souls. Yet, there are believers today who believe in we should pray for the dead so that they can be given a second chance, or their sins may be forgiven as they go through purgatory. This doctrine is taught in the Apocrypha. 2 Maccabees 12:46 reads, "Thus he made atonement for the dead that they might be freed from this sin."

If the unbelieving dead may be given a second chance, it would make the Great Commission meaningless. Why should we evangelize since we can pray for their second chance?

The doctrine of praying for the dead is not from the Scripture. Care for the living now before it is too late.

Baptizing for the Dead?

1 Corinthians 15:29 reads, *"Now if there is no resurrection, what will those do who are baptized for the dead? If the dead are not raised at all, why are people baptized for them?"* The Mormon Church practices baptizing for the dead based on this verse, and the declaration of Joseph Smith.[126] This is

---

[126]Mormonism believes that no one can enter the "celestial" heaven without being baptized. But those who have died can gain admittance if others are baptized for them. The Book of Mormon never mentions the doctrine, but it is declared by Joseph Smith, 'The greatest...commandment given us, and

"proxy" or "vicarious" baptism. This is a wrong interpretation of the verse.

Paul is not advocating the baptism of the living on behalf of the dead. He is using the current practice of his day to argue the point that there is a belief in the resurrection. A few people of his day were baptizing for the dead because they believe that the dead will be resurrected if the living were baptized vicariously for the dead.

I often find Christians suffering from two defective ways of argument. The first is to argue from the right premise but ends with the wrong conclusion. This argument is used by Paul in Romans 6:1 *"What shall we say, then? Shall we go on sinning so that grace may increase?"* The right premise is the abundance of the grace of God in forgiving sinners. The wrong conclusion would be to continue sinning (so that grace may increase). To argue that since there is an abundance of His grace (right premise), we can continue to sin against God (wrong conclusion) would be contrary to the doctrine of the grace of God.

The second defective argument is the reverse of the first. It starts from a wrong premise, but (strangely enough) it ends with a right conclusion. This is exactly what happens in 1 Corinthians 15:29. The conclusion is right: There will be resurrection. But the argument comes from a wrong premise: Baptize the dead. Paul therefore is affirming their right conclusion without affirming their wrong premise.

There is no evidence that the early church ever practiced baptizing for the dead for the salvation and consequent

---

made obligatory, is the temple work in our own behalf and in behalf of our dead.' "

> resurrection of the dead. Salvation is by grace through faith in Jesus Christ. No living person can give salvation to another living or dead persons. For a person to be saved, he/she must come to faith in Christ, and Christ alone, without works. Do not delay coming to Him. Do not wait for someone to be baptized for you after you are dead. It wouldn't help!

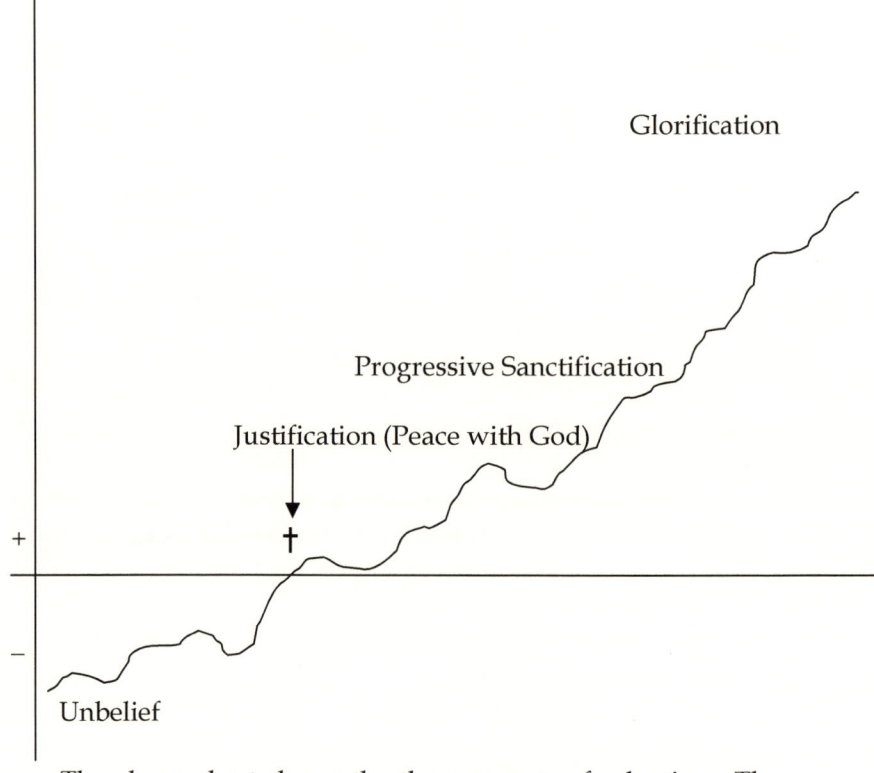

[Chart showing three aspects of salvation: Unbelief in the (-) section, Justification (Peace with God) marked with a cross at the crossing point, Progressive Sanctification rising upward, leading to Glorification.]

The above chart shows the three aspects of salvation. The line at the (-) section shows that the person is still an unbeliever. He/she comes to know Christ when he/she crosses the line into the (+) section. What follows, hopefully, is an upward journey of spiritual growth even though there may be valleys. Ultimately, upon death, the believer enters into His glory.

Heaven vs. Nirvana

Heaven is not the same as Nirvana. Nirvana is the extinction of all desires. It is a state of "nothingness." The person is forever free from the cycle of rebirth. After all the cycles of rebirth, and having eliminated all desires, a person arrived at "nothing" – Nirvana.

Nirvana is NOT a state of existence. Heaven, however, "is a final state of existence where individual identity is maintained and will continue eternally. Death is not the dissolution of personality, but a state of fuller existence."[127] Heaven is not a state of nothingness. Heaven is where God dwells, and we are in the presence of the Almighty.

Heaven is not something man can create for himself, like Nirvana, but something that God creates for man.[128]

In Nirvana, there is an escape from existence itself. A person escapes from existence into non-existence. But a Christian plunges into the fullness of existence in heaven upon death. The Kingdom is not a distant goal, but a present reality. In this life, I can have His life.[129]

Which one would you prefer? Nirvana or Heaven? Buddha or Christ?

---

[127]Tissa Weerasingha, *TheCross & the Bo Tree,* p. 42.
[128]Ibid.
[129]Ibid.

Requirement for salvation

Acts 16:31 says: *"Believe in the Lord Jesus, and you will be saved...."* Salvation is obtained through faith in Christ, requiring nothing else (Eph. 2:8, cf. John 3:16, 36; 5:25; 20:31). It is justification by faith alone *(sola fide)*. It is a gift of God. The only requirement for salvation is belief in the Lord Jesus. Salvation is extended to those who believe in Christ.

1. Salvation is not gained through repentance, in the sense that you have to turn from sin or to change your conduct before you can be saved. If we need to change our conduct or turn from sin before we can be saved, salvation is no longer of grace but of works.

    The basic meaning of repentance is "to change one's mind or attitude." The object of repentance is determined by the context. The object of repentance may be dead works (Heb. 6:1), or Christ (i.e. changing your mind or attitude concerning Jesus Christ [Acts 2:38]), or God (i.e. changing your mind or attitude concerning God [Acts 17:30, 20:21]), or sin (Acts 8:22). God wishes for everyone to change their minds or attitudes and to consider seriously the consequences about the future day of judgment (2 Peter 3:9).

    Salvation is, therefore, not gained through repentance in the sense that you have to turn from sin or to change your conduct before you can be saved, but salvation involves repentance in the sense of changing your mind or attitude toward God, Christ, dead works or sin. When a person believes Christ, his mind or attitude definitely changes toward God, Christ, dead works or sin. Otherwise, he would not believe in Christ at all.

2. Salvation is not gained by obedience, in the sense of obeying (or trying to obey) all the commands of Jesus Christ (other than the command to believe Him [1 John 3:23][130]). Again, if obedience to the commands of Jesus Christ is required for salvation, our salvation is of works, not of grace.

3. Salvation is not gained by "making" Christ the Lord of our lives. (I am not suggesting Christ is not the Lord.) Mistakes are sometimes made during evangelistic meetings by indicating we must "make" Him the Lord of our lives or we must "surrender" our lives to Him before we can be saved. If we need to "make" Him the Lord of our lives or to "surrender" our lives to Him *before* we can be saved, salvation is again of works, not of grace.

We believe in the *Lord* Jesus Christ for our salvation. The word "Lord" means Jesus Christ is God. The term indicates His position as the Deity. When we believe in the Lord Jesus Christ, we believe He is God. We believe He has the ability to save us. But this is different from saying you need to straighten out your life or to surrender your life in order to be saved. I am not saying we should live careless lives after we are saved. But we should surrender our lives, commit our lives to Him, let Him change our lives into His likeness *after* we are saved. Those fruits come *after* our salvation, not *before* our salvation.

---

[130]We are commanded to believe in Jesus Christ. Refusal to believe Christ is an act of disobedience. We are to obey the command to believe. That does not mean that obedience to "all the commands" of Christ is needed for salvation. The only command is to believe in Jesus Christ for salvation.

4. Salvation is not gained by baptism. Baptism follows conversion as an act of obedience to His command, but it is not a requirement for salvation. Those who argued for the need of baptism for salvation usually point to Acts 2:38: *Repent and be baptized, every one of you, in the name of Jesus Christ for the forgiveness of your sins. And you will receive the gift of the Holy Spirit.* But this verse does not support baptismal salvation. This passage should be translated more accurately as "Repent (and be baptized, every one of you), in the name of Jesus Christ for the forgiveness of your sins. And you will receive the gift of the Holy Spirit." This translation puts the requirement for baptism in the parenthesis.[131] Baptism then becomes an accompaniment of repentance, not a requirement of salvation. Peter did not add "baptism" in his future speeches in Acts 3:19, 5:31, 10:43 (cf. Luke 3:3, 24:47).

5. Salvation is not gained by works.[132] When the rich young ruler asked Jesus, "What must I do to inherit eternal life?" (Luke 18:18), Jesus told him to sell everything he had and to give them to the poor. Is Christ saying to him to work for his salvation? No. The issue facing the rich young ruler was trusting in his own wealth. He needed to transfer his trust on wealth to Christ. The ruler had a problem believing in Christ. His wealth was a stumbling block.

6. Salvation is not through purgatory. The doctrine of purgatory contradicts the Scripture, diminishes the grace of God, and is an insult to the *finished* work of Christ on the Cross. If we have to go through purgatory, salvation

---

[131]This is a better translation because it takes into consideration the changes from the plural (repent, your sins) to singular (baptized, every one of you).
[132]The Roman Catholic's Council of Trent pronounced the necessity of good works for ultimate justification.

is through human effort, and that Christ's death on the Cross is insufficient for our salvation.

7. Salvation is not by sacraments. According to the Roman Catholic dogma, salvation is by partaking the sacraments because they impart the grace of God upon sinners. This dogma is contrary to the teaching of the Scripture.

8. Salvation is not working hard in this life in order to pay off one's "karmic debt," thereby securing a better position in the next life.

Salvation is, therefore, a gift to receive, not a goal to achieve. It is the grace of God, not the works of man/woman, lest anyone should boast (Eph. 2:8-9). The grace of God must never be minimized in the doctrine of salvation. We bring nothing to the cross. We can contribute nothing to the finished work of Christ. We did nothing to merit salvation. Protestants believe in the *exclusivity* of grace, i.e. grace alone (*sola gratia*) apart from any good works. "The distinguishing salvation doctrines of the Reformation, then, are grace alone and faith alone (*sola gratia* and *sola fide*) through Christ alone and based on the Bible alone."[133]

The *bhakti* movement originated in south India that seems to view salvation as only through grace, but the *bhakti* conceived grace differently from the Christian sense. Bruce Nicholls clarifies,

> ... it is a method to merit the grace of God. Grace operates within the framework of the law of *karma* and *dharma* (duty). It does not cancel it. In Christianity grace

---

[133]Norman L. Geisler & Ralph MacKenzie, *Roman Catholics and Evangelicals*, p. 221.

cancels the works of the law; but in Hinduism it hastens the process of deliverance from bondage to *karma* and the wheel of rebirth. The god Siva who is always associated with grace never annuls *dharma*, but guides the soul more quickly through it.[134]

Sunil H. Stephens adds,

The grace-slanted *bhakti* school proposes salvation through grace alone, without the cross of Calvary. Since all must pay for their own *karma*, then there is no room for anyone else to take upon oneself other's *karma*. Nevertheless, this is exactly what Jesus did: He took upon Himself our bad *karma* and in exchange gave us His good *karma*.[135]

Exclusivity of Salvation

The doctrine of universalism believes that all will be saved is unscriptural. Not all will be saved, but only those who trusted Christ.

The Bible is clear on the necessity of the precise knowledge of Christ for salvation. *"Salvation is found in no one else, for there is no other name under heaven given to men by which we must be saved"* (Acts 4:12) is the *exclusive* claim of Scripture. There is no salvation apart from Jesus Christ. Jesus is the *only* Way, Truth and Life. He is not one of the many ways to salvation.

---

[134] Bruce J. Nichols, "Hinduism," *The World's Religions,* ed. Norman Anderson (London: Inter Varsity, 1950; repr. Grand Rapids: Eerdmans, 1983, pp. 136-68 [147]). Quoted in Sunil H. Stephens, "Doing Theology in a Hindu Context," *Journal of Asian Mission* (1/2, 1999): 191-92.

[135] Sunil H. Stephens, "Doing Theology in a Hindu Context," *Journal of Asian Mission* (1/2, 1999): 192.

Results of salvation

When a person believes in Christ, several things happen simultaneously:

1. **Justification** (Rom. 4:25, 5:9, 16, 18; Gal. 2:16): Justification is an act of God where He forensically *declares* the sinner righteous[136] because of the sinner's trust in Christ based on His finished work on the cross. This *declaration* is often known as *extrinsic* justification[137] as opposed to *intrinsic* justification. Intrinsic justification means that a person is *made* righteous by God's grace.

   In justification, the believer secures...

   a. Peace with God: There is peace with God, Christ having removed the enmity between God and man/woman (Rom. 5:1; Eph. 2:14).

   b. Forgiveness of sins (Acts 13:38; Rom. 4:7-8; Eph. 1:7, 4:32; Col. 2:13): There is no condemnation (Rom. 8:1, 33) because He bore our sins on the cross (Isa. 53:5-6; 1 Pet. 2:24).

> Many of the Eastern religions believe in re-incarnations through the uncountable cycles of rebirth in order to ultimately achieve Nirvana or merge into the universal One. It is human effort to

---

[136] Righteous in the forensic sense (legal standpoint).

[137] Contrary to the Protestant doctrine of extrinsic justification, the Roman Catholic's Council of Trent defined justification in terms of a man *becoming* righteous. Paul used the word *dikaioó* (to justified) in a forensic or legal sense. To justify is to *declare* a person righteous.

> liberate oneself from the bondage to the law of *karma*.
>
> The Christian gospel is good news. First, it is a gift of God. Salvation is a gift to receive not a goal to achieve. It is not man seeking to liberate himself, but Christ seeking and saving sinners. Second, "instead of a cycle of existence which LEADS to emancipation ultimately, what the Christian Gospel offers is a new birth now which BEGINS an emancipated existence."[138] Praise the Lord.

2. **Imputation of the righteousness of Christ** (2 Cor. 5:21; James 2:23): God imputed the righteousness of Christ to believers so we can have fellowship with Him.

3. **Regeneration**: Regeneration is the impartation of divine life to the believer (John 3:16, 36, 10:28; 1 John 5:11; 2 Pet. 1:4; 2 Cor. 5:17).

4. **Adoption:** The believer is adopted as a child of God into the family of God (Rom. 8:15, 23; Gal. 4:5; Eph. 1:5). Furthermore, the believer is made an heir of God and a co-heir with Christ (Rom. 8:16; Gal. 3:26; Heb. 2:11).

5. **Sealing of the Holy Spirit** (Eph. 1:13): The believer is sealed with the Holy Spirit. If anyone does not have the Spirit of Christ, he does not belong to Christ (Rom. 8:9).

6. **Union with Christ**: Believers are "in" Christ, united with Him spiritually (John 14:20; Rom. 6:11, 8:1; 2 Cor. 5:17; Eph. 2:13; Col. 2:11-13; Gal. 3:27; 1 John 4:13). One's personality is retained in this union with Christ.

---

[138]Tissa Weerasingha, *The Cross & the Bo Tree*, p. 34.

Your personality and your own self are not lost in this union. This union is different from the doctrine of union as taught by Hinduism where a person *merges* into the Brahman and *loses* himself in it, "like a drop absorbed in the ocean."[139]

7. **Baptism into His Body**: The believer is baptized into His Body, the universal Church (1 Cor. 12:13). The believer becomes a member of the family of God worldwide.

8. **Begins the process of sanctification**: Sanctification is the continuing process of being set apart from the world to God so believers will become more Christ-like (1 Pet. 1:16). A believer is *declared* righteous at justification, but *made* righteous in sanctification. Both justification and sanctification are by His grace. The means of justification also determines the means of sanctification. If we are justified by grace, we are also sanctified by grace (Rom. 5:1-2).

"Buddhism and the New Testament Gospel stand poles apart. While the one stands for annihilation and negation of life, the other stands for new creation and abundant life. One stands for denial of existence, the other for affirmation of meaningful existence. One aims to abolish the earth and the heavens, the other stands for a new earth and a new heaven. One stands for denial of self, the other stands for sublimation of the self. One sanctions escape from the endless cycle of life in time and space, the other stands for pre-determined eschatological redemption of time, space and matter. One tries to move from despair to stoic serenity, the other moves with certainty and confidence from battle to glory. One moves into the sphere of inaction, the other moves into the intensity of purposeful action. One sees

---

[139] E. Ahmad-Shah, *Theology – Christian and Hindu*, p. 80.

> endless suffering as the only reality, the other sees glory in suffering as meaningful reality. Thus Jainism and Buddhism totally fail to meet the desperate need of man in all the different situations of life."[140]

Assurance of salvation

There are two main views on the security of believers:

1. Salvation cannot be lost. Once saved, always saved. The believer is eternally secure. The power of God is able to keep the believer in His hand. Jesus said, *"I give them eternal life, and they shall never perish; no one can snatch them out of my hand"* (John 10:28). If salvation may be lost, it diminishes the keeping power of God, and it will depend on our own effort to keep the gift -- that would be salvation by works.

   Romans 5:6-11 is a crucial passage on salvation.

   > *You see, at just the right time, when we were still powerless, Christ died for the ungodly. Very rarely will anyone die for a righteous man, though for a good man someone might possibly dare to die. But God demonstrates his own love for us in this: While we were still sinners, Christ died for us. Since we have now been justified by his blood, how much more shall we be saved from God's wrath through him! For if, when we were God's enemies, we were reconciled to him through the death of his Son, how much more, having been reconciled, shall we be saved through his life! Not only is this so, but we also rejoice in God through our Lord Jesus Christ, through whom we have now received reconciliation.*

   Christ died for us while we were ...
   - Powerless,

---

[140] Paul Pillai, *India's Search for the Unknown Christ*, p. 57.

- Ungodly, and
- Sinful.

The argument that Paul put forth is that if Christ died for us while we were still sinners, would He not keep us until the end? Paul uses the words, "how much more" twice (vs. 9, 10) to emphasize his point. Suppose that you were my enemies, and I did all the nice things to you while you were my enemies, wouldn't I continue to count on your friendship when we are now reconciled as friends? If I did all the nice things to you while you were my enemy, wouldn't you be able to count on me now we have become friends? Indeed, much more. If I love you while you were my enemy, *much more* would I love you now we are friends! If Christ died for us while we were His enemies, *much more* He shall keep us safe through His life when we have been reconciled to Him!

2. On the other hand, other believers, while believing that the salvation of Christ is certain and assured as we trust Him, argue that salvation may be lost if you willfully leave Christ, deny Him, literally trample His blood under your feet, curse Him, and turn your back against Christ (Heb. 6:4-8). It does not mean that you lose your salvation every time you sin, but there is the possibility of losing one's salvation for willful disobedience to Him.

Wonderful believers and heroes of faith on both sides of this issue have argued for their positions.

Sunil H. Stephens calls the above two schools: the cat school, and the monkey school. The cat school refers to the kitten being carried by the mouth of its mother. The mother assures that the kitten will not be dropped. This is Calvinism. The monkey school says that the baby monkey *has* to cling to the mother. If the baby monkey does not cling to the mother, the baby monkey will be dropped. This is Armenianism.[141] (I prefer to be the kitten!)

Greatness of our salvation

We have a glorious salvation:

1 Peter 1:1-5: *Peter, an apostle of Jesus Christ, To God's elect, strangers in the world, scattered throughout Pontus, Galatia, Cappadocia, Asia and Bithynia, who have been chosen according to the foreknowledge of God the Father, through the sanctifying work of the Spirit, for obedience to Jesus Christ and sprinkling by his blood: Grace and peace be yours in abundance. Praise be to the God and Father of our Lord Jesus Christ! In his great mercy he has given us new birth into a living hope through the resurrection of Jesus Christ from the dead, and into an inheritance that can never perish, spoil or fade-- kept in heaven for you, who through faith are shielded by God's power until the coming of the salvation that is ready to be revealed in the last time.*

We praise the Lord for the greatness of our salvation because we have:

1. Promise of a living hope. *"He has given us new birth into a living hope."*
2. Perpetual inheritance. *"An inheritance that can never perish, spoil or fade."*
3. Protection by the power of God. *"Kept in heaven for you, who through faith are shielded by God's power until the coming of the salvation that is ready to be revealed in the last time."*

Rejoice and be glad!

---

[141] Sunil H. Stephens, "Doing Theology in a Hindu Context," *Journal of Asian Mission* (1/2, 1999):190.

Applications

1. Write down the names of four non-Christians and begin praying daily for them to come to know Christ.

2. Rejoice at your new birth, but don't stop there. Too many have been saved and "stuck" or stunted in their spiritual growth. Pursue spiritual growth vigorously and eagerly. What are your plans to grow spiritually this year?

Questions

1. Is there a blasphemy of the Holy Spirit today?

2. Do babies who die go to heaven?

The Doctrine of the Church (Ecclesiology)

Objective

To understand the doctrine of the church and to renew our commitment to the local church in fulfilling God's purpose on earth.

Definition

1. The church (*ekklesia*) is the "call-out ones" of God. The word *ekklesia* is a compound word taken from *kaleo* "to call," and *ek*, "out from." The word *ekklesia* means "the call-out ones." As the word refers to the church, it means a people called out from the world to be a people of God, a royal priesthood (1 Pet. 2:5, 9; Rev. 1:6, 5:10), the bride of Christ (2 Cor. 11:2; Matt. 25:6), the household of God (Eph. 2:19), the flock of God (John 10:1-29; 1 Pet. 5:3-4; Heb. 13:20; Acts 20:28), and the

temple of God (Eph. 2:21-22; 1 Cor. 3:9, 16; 1 Tim. 3:15; 1 Pet. 2:5).

2. The church is the mystery of God hidden in the Old, but revealed in the New (Matt. 16:18; Rom. 11:25, 16:25; Eph. 3:9). It is a new creation (Matt. 9:17; Eph. 2:15).

3. The church is not a continuation of Israel or the abrogation of Israel. The national promises to Israel (such as the land) will be fulfilled to the nation, not to the church (Rom. 9-11). Israel is national and geographical, the church is spiritual and international, comprised of believing Jews and Gentiles.

4. The church is not a building. Christ said He would build His church (singular, universal) (Matt. 16:18).

5. The church is "that body of people which has been called unto God by means of the gospel of Jesus Christ, brought into a life relationship with Jesus Christ by faith, and baptized into the body of Jesus Christ by the Holy Spirit. It is the temple of God indwelt by the Holy Spirit, constituting a brotherhood in the household of God, a peculiar people to serve a unique purpose of God in this age with a blessed hope of occupying a unique position with the Lord in the ages to come."[142] The church therefore is an invisible mystical body.[143]

6. The church is multi-cultural, multiethnic, multiracial, trans-gender, trans-social-ranking, trans-generational, trans-national, and trans-linguistic. It is not limited to

---

[142]George W Peters, *A Biblical Theology of Missions* (Chicago, IL: Moody Press, 1972), p. 202.

[143]The Roman Catholics believe that the church is not merely an invisible mystical body but also a visible organization on earth whose headquarters is in Rome.

only one culture, ethnic group, race, gender, social ranking, generation, caste, nation or language. God calls people to become His own children from all cultures, ethnicities, nations, and languages. The come from *every nation, tribe, people and language* (Rev. 7:9). He calls peoples from all walks of life, social rankings (rich, and poor, and the not so poor), castes, men, women, all generations (children, teens, adults, the elderly). He calls the Jews and the Gentiles. He calls Indians, and also Eurasians, the Portuguese and also the Chinese. Our God is not a tribal God, and the church of God is not a tribal church. It is a universal church, transcending all cultural, ethnic, racial, gender, social, generational, national, and language barriers (Gal. 3:28).

7. The word "church" may also be used in a local sense (Acts 8:1; 11:2; 1 Cor. 1:2; 2 Cor. 1:1; Gal. 1:2) when it refers to believers who gather together to carry out the mission of the church. George Peters defines the local church as that ordered body of professing believers who, "on the basis of common experiences of the Lord and convictions of the Word, in the bond of mutual love and understanding, in the interest of common concerns and causes, and for the purposes of mutual spiritual benefits and fellowship, assemble themselves together according to the Word of God, conduct worship services in an organized and orderly manner, observe the Lord's ordinances, perform such functions as they deem advantageous to themselves and their community according to the Word of God, and discharge such other responsibilities as they judge their duty before God and man."[144]

---

[144] Ibid.

8. The church is built by Christ. Jesus said He would build His church (Matt. 16:18). It is the workmanship of God (Eph. 2:10). Paul said the church rests upon the foundation of Jesus Christ (1 Cor. 3:11).

9. The church is preserved by Christ. Jesus promised, *"The gates of Hades will not overcome it."* (Matt 16:18) He promised His protection. Men have tried to destroy the church, but to no avail.

10. The church is God's possession (1 Pet. 2:9, 1 Cor. 6:19-20). The church is the household *of* God (denoting possession) (Eph. 2:9), the flock *of* God (John 10:1-29; 1 Pet. 5:3-4; Heb. 13:20; Acts 20:28), and the bride *of* Christ (2 Cor. 11:2; Matt. 25:6).

11. The church is not an institution of salvation. Based on a faulty interpretation of the Scripture, and argument from traditions, the Roman Catholics believe that the church is an institution of salvation which dispenses grace a portion at a time by the seven sacraments from birth to death through the priesthood.[145]

The Founding of the Church

The church was founded on the day of Pentecost (Acts 2) with the coming of the Spirit to perform (among other works) its special task of baptizing believers into one body, the body of Christ (1 Cor. 12:13). The church, therefore, is founded on Christ, formed by the Spirit and inaugurated on the day of Pentecost.

---

[145]Norman L. Geisler & Ralph E. MacKenzie, *Roman Catholics and Evangelicals*, p. 285.

The mission[146] of the local church

1. Worship: The primary objective of the church's call is to praise the glory of God's grace (Eph. 1:6; 1 Pet. 2:5).

2. Instruction: Jesus commanded the disciples to teach believers to obey everything He commanded (Matt. 28:20 cf. 2 Tim. 2:2). The disciples taught the believers after they believed in Christ (Acts 2:42-47, 12:21-22). Christ also gave teachers to the church to *"prepare God's people for works of service, so that the body of Christ may be built up until we all reach unity in the faith and in the knowledge of the Son of God and become mature, attaining to the whole measure of the fullness of Christ."* (Eph. 4:12-13)

3. Fellowship: The fellowship is both spiritual and physical. Spiritual fellowship would include sharing hearts together around the Word, and physical fellowship would be meeting the physical needs of members of God's family. These dual aspects are brought out clearly in Acts 2:42-47. They were learning and sharing the Word. And they were also sharing material things and ministering to those in need. Christians are called into the fellowship of God the Father (1 John 1:3), of His Son Jesus Christ (1 Cor. 1:9), and of the Holy Spirit (2 Cor. 13:14). Christians are to

---

[146]There is always confusion between "mission" (singular) and "missions" (plural). George Peters provides a good differentiation: "Mission" refers to the total biblical assignment of the church of Jesus Christ. It is a comprehensive term including the upward, inward and outward ministries of the church. "Missions" is a specialized term. It refers to the sending forth of authorized persons beyond the borders of the New Testament church and her immediate gospel influence to proclaim the gospel of Jesus Christ in gospel-destitute areas, to win converts from other faiths or non-faiths to Jesus Christ, and to establish functioning, multiplying local congregations who will bear the fruit of Christianity in that community and to that country. (*A Biblical Theology of Missions*, p. 11.)

come together to consider how we may spur one another on toward love and good deeds (Heb. 10:24-25). Believers are to show hospitality to strangers (Heb. 13:1-3) and to visit orphans and widows in their distress (James 1:27). Luke ministered to Paul's physical health (2 Tim. 4:11). The church in Philippi ministered to the material need of Paul (Phil. 4:6). The Corinthian church helped the poor saints of Jerusalem (Rom. 15:25-27; 1 Cor. 16:3; 2 Cor. 8:9). The early believers ministered to the widows (Acts 6:1).

4. Evangelism: The Great Commission is to be fulfilled by the church (Matt. 28:18-20; Mark 16:15-16; Luke 24:46-49; John 20:21; Acts 1:8). The central command of the Great Commission in Matthew 28:18-20 is, "make disciples." The supporting participles -- "going," "baptizing," and "teaching" delineate the process of making disciples.

The government of the local church

The universal church is an *organism,* but the local church (a group of believers) has to be *organized* so it can carry out the various functions of the church.

1. **The principles of church government**:

    a. The church leaders are faithful in understanding, living and teaching the Word (Acts 2:42; 1 Tim. 3:2; 1 Peter 5:1-5; Titus 1:9).

    b. The church leaders have spiritual maturity, godly character (1 Tim. 3:1-16).

    c. Church leaders are appointed, not because of their spiritual gifts, but because of their spiritual qualifications (1 Tim. 3:1-16). It is dangerous and dishonoring to the Lord to appoint leaders for their outstanding demonstration or display of their gifts without the foundation of godly character. Many churches have been ruined because they mistook the scaffoldings as the real building!

d. The church leaders are to shepherd the flock voluntarily, eagerly, and not because of duty, material gain or craving for dominance (1 Peter 5:1-3; Acts 20:28; 1 Tim. 3:2; Titus 1:9).

e. The church has team leadership. The terms elders and overseers always appear in the plural in the New Testament. Plurality of leaders seemed to be the norm in the New Testament (Acts 2:42-43; 1 Thess. 5:12-13; Heb. 13:17). The "one man" ministry is fraught with many dangers. This does not mean there should not be a senior pastor, but it means he should work in a team (even though he is leading it and should be a godly example to the team members). A group of elders or deacons or a pastoral team, working together, will complete what is lacking in him. No one person is given all the gifts necessary for the work of the church. We need the other members of the body to complement one another.

f. The church has the involvement of the leaders and the laity together. The church is not to be run by one person or a group of leaders, but rather all believers are to serve as ministers, involved in Christ's ministry (1 Cor. 12; 1 Peter 2:1-10).

g. The church has a harmonious and orderly structure. Paul wrote to the Corinthian church that "God is not a God of disorder but of peace" (1 Cor. 14:33), and "everything should be done in a fitting and orderly way" (1 Cor. 14:40). Paul instructed Titus to "straighten out" the things in the churches in Crete (Titus 1:5). Paul wrote to Timothy so people would know how to conduct themselves (1 Tim. 3:15).

2. **The form of church government**: The New Testament prescribes no specific form of church government. The manner in which churches are organized are left to the discretion of the local group of believers under the guidance of the Holy Spirit, provided the church is faithful to His Word, has godly leadership, and fulfills the mission (function) of the church. Assuming the church is faithful to His Word and has godly leadership, the *function* of the local church will determine the *form* of church government. *Form* follows *function*. The problem with many churches is that to lock into (or worst still, to absolutize) a particular *form* of church government may not be effective in accomplishing its *function*. The function of the church (described in a previous section) may have certain unique features in a certain locality that may require a different *form* of church government (or organization) so it can be more effective in its ministry. The *form* of church government is *not* an absolute. It can be changed so that it best accomplishes its mission in your city. The *form* is a means to the end. Unfortunately, many churches consider the *form* the end! Keep the church government simple and flexible. Keep the proper focus: to accomplish His mission, not to perpetuate the organization. If the organization is no longer effective in accomplishing His mission, please be willing to change!

3. **The officers of the church**:

    a. Apostles: The term is applied primarily to the eleven disciples who were with Christ during His public ministry (Matt. 10:2; Acts 1:26). It was also apply to Paul (Gal. 1:1; 1 Cor. 9:1; 2 Cor. 12:12) and other men in the New Testament who were "sent": Barnabas (Acts 14:14), Timothy, Silvanus (1 Thess. 2:6-7), Andronicus and Junias (Rom. 16:7). The apostles laid the foundation of the church (Eph. 2:20).

b. Prophet: The term is applied to the four daughters of the evangelist Philip, to Agabus (Acts 21) and to the persons who spoke as the Holy Spirit moved them (Acts 11:28, 13:12, 15:32; 1 Cor. 12:10, 13:2, 14:3; Eph. 2:20, 3:5, 4:1; 1 Tim. 1:18, 4:14; Rev. 11:6). The prophets assisted the apostles and laid the foundation of the church (Eph. 2:20).

c. Pastors, Bishops, Elders: These three terms denote the same person or office (1 Pet. 5:1-2; Acts 20). Paul used the words, elders and overseers, interchangeably (Acts 20:17; Titus 1:5, 7; 1 Tim. 3:1-2, 5:17-19). They were to feed the flock (1 Pet. 5:1-2), represent the whole church (Acts 15:6, 20:28), share in the ministry (Acts 11:30), care for the believers (James 5:14), teach (Titus 1:9) and see that all things were done in order (Titus 1:5; 1 Cor. 14:40).

d. Deacons: The term is used to describe the ones who serve (Matt. 20:26, 22:13; Phil. 1:1; 1 Tim. 3:8, 12) and, more specifically, to the seven men chosen to minister to the poor widows (Acts 6:1-6). They were involved in relief ministries.

e. Deaconess: The term is applied to Phoebe in the church of Cenchrea (Rom. 16:1). Deaconess possibly assisted deacons in the various duties of the church.

A word, however, needs to be said concerning the various titles of the officers of the church. We should not be locked into certain titles. The titles are non-absolutes. More importantly, the various offices are responsible to fulfilling the church mission. Titles can be changed. There is nothing in the Bible that prohibits us from changing the titles. I agree with Gene Getz who says:

"Paul demonstrated this principle clearly. He did not hesitate to use more than one title in order to communicate the meaning or idea behind a leadership position in the church. To the Christians converted out of the Greek culture, the term, "bishop" had significant meaning when talking about church leadership. To the Jewish Christians, the term, "elder" was obvious and clear. But both were "good" words to describe those who were to lead the local churches in the New Testament.

"It is also obvious that the Holy Spirit allowed Paul to borrow words from both the religious and secular cultures that surrounded these people. It was not necessary to come up with a word that was uniquely "Christian." Though an "elder" in Israel performed a leadership functions within Judaism and a "bishop" served in the secular community as an overseer of certain colonies, both words could be used to adequately describe the "overseer" of a local church. "The important point, of course, is that the person needed to be *uniquely* qualified to oversee this *new* and *distinctive* group of people. Today the twentieth century church does not need to get "locked in" to titles and "terminologies." We should be free to select and choose titles that will clearly describe New Testament functions in the twentieth century."[147]

---

[147] Gene A. Getz, *Sharpening the Focus of the Church* (Chicago, IL: Moody Press, 1974), pp. 128-29.

The role of women in the church

The role of the women in the church has provoked lively debates and, on occasions, given rise to hard feelings on both sides. Unfortunately, it has also led to divisions in the church. It is as if men and women entered into the arena and came out badly bruised.

There are various positions held by contemporary church leaders. On one extreme, the male-dominated leadership insists woman are to keep silent in the church without any right to speak—and don't think about leading at all! They are quick to point to 1 Corinthians 14:33-35 to support their position. On the other extreme are others who advocate ordaining woman and lesbians into the ministry. It is impossible to deal with this "hot" topic in this book, but I want to propose a few guidelines for you to think about.

1. The role of women (and men) must be discussed in the broader context of the ministry of the local church. First, the local church must determine its mission. Why do you have the church in this location? Why has God called you together? What is the purpose of your church? This is the most foundational question you have to think through. Be very specific in nailing down the mission or purpose of your church.

    After you have determined the purpose of your church, then the various *programs* must flow out of that *purpose*. Programs come after purpose. Programs must be purpose-driven. Unfortunately, there are many programs in the church without any specific purpose at all.

After you have determined the *purpose* and *programs*, then you can decide on the *personnel*. Who are the people God has brought to your church to carry out the various programs to fulfill the purpose of the church? Now pray, and evaluate those who come to the church, men or women whom God has called (and some, gifted), to fill the various positions in the church. If God, for example, has definitely called and gifted a woman in the church to take care of accounting, there is nothing that prohibits her to be the church accountant. You will have to decide on the organizational structure that best suits your church. God blesses both men and women with various gifts. We want to be faithful in utilizing the gifts God has given to the church. In what ways can we best utilize the gifts He has given to women in the church?

What I am saying is, the role of the women in the church ought to be discussed within the broader framework of the purpose (mission) of the church. Dealing with just the role of the women in the church by itself is a piecemeal solution.

Diagrammatically, I illustrate the process as follows:

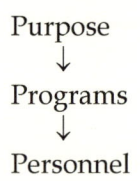

$$\text{Purpose} \\ \downarrow \\ \text{Programs} \\ \downarrow \\ \text{Personnel}$$

2. The leaders of the church must recognize the godliness and the gifting of God to women, and seek to maximize their potential, according to the best understanding and application of the biblical texts.

3. Both men and women are to have a quiet, submissive and gentle spirit before God and toward one another, and always seek to maintain the unity and harmony of His church as a testimony to the outside world.

4. When individuals and churches whose conscientious understanding of the Bible concerning the role of the women in the church differ from yours, continue to love one another without endorsing extreme practices contrary to the Word of God.

The ordinances of the church

Protestants believe that Christ instituted only two ordinances: Baptism and the Lord's Supper.[148]

1. Baptism:

   a. Baptism was instituted by Christ (Matt. 28:19-20) and practiced by the early church (Acts 2:38, 41, 8:12, 36-38, 9:18, 10:47, 16:14-15, 33, 18:8, 19:5).

   b. Baptism means identification with Christ. The baptismal act signifies the believer's death to the old life and his resurrection as a new creature in union with Christ (Rom. 6:4; Col. 2:12).[149]

   c. Baptism does not confer the grace of justification. The Roman Catholic Church believes that baptism confers the grace of justification (baptismal

---

[148] The Roman Catholic Church practices seven sacraments – baptism, confirmation, Eucharist, penance, extreme unction, holy order, and matrimony.

[149] Baptism does not mean that the believer ceases to be a member of his own society as many non-believers mistakenly believed, and hence vehemently oppose baptism, and persecute even their own family members when they become followers of Christ.

regeneration). This is contrary to the doctrine of salvation by grace alone through faith alone.

d. There is much debate on the mode of baptism. In the New Testament, although the verb generally implies immersion, it doesn't necessarily need to do so. For example, in Luke 11:38 the Greek term *ebaptistha* (baptism) was used to describe the Pharisaic practice of washing the hands before meals. The Pharisees wondered if Jesus had washed (*ebaptistha*) before dinner. But such a washing would not have been by immersing the hands in water, but rather by having water poured over them. The parallel passage in Mark 7:4 uses the verb *rhantizein*, which means to "sprinkle."[150] The preposition "in" (Greek, *eis*, "into") and "out " (*ek*) do not necessarily indicate immersion. In Acts 8:38-39 both Philip and the Ethiopian went into (*eis*) the water and came out (*ek*). But it does not indicate that they went into the water, which may be implying something more like pouring.[151] Believers of baptism by immersion only often point to the practice of John the Baptist in the Gospels. But the argument from the Gospel records is fraught with hermeneutical problems. Hermeneutically, the *description* is not a *prescription* for *repetition*, so, we cannot argue from the descriptive portions of the Scripture to prescribe what must be done today. Otherwise, we would have to insist on having all baptisms in River Jordan to be truly biblical!

Even though baptism was generally and characteristically administered by immersion by the

---

[150] James Keir Howard, *New Testament Baptism* (London, UK: Pickering and Inglis, 1970), p. 47.
[151] Robert L. Saucy, *The Church in God's Program*, p. 210.

early church, the baptismal mode is again a non-absolute. While immersion best pictures the identification with Christ in His death and resurrection and should be preferred, one should not hold to this mode with an ironclad inflexibility — especially when circumstances do not permit this mode. The *meaning* of baptism is more important than the *mode* of baptism.

A word of caution: If your church practices a different mode of baptism than you have been taught to believe, please respect its tradition and do not use this issue to cause chaos or division in the church. There are more important issues for you to be concerned about. By all means, preserve the unity of the church for a vibrant testimony to the outside world.

2. The Lord's Supper:

   a. The Lord's Supper was instituted by Christ before His death (Matt. 26:26-29; Mark 14:22-25; Luke 22:17-20), confirmed by Paul (1 Cor. 11:23-26) and practiced by the early church (1 Cor. 11:23; Acts 2:42, 46, 20:7, 11).

   b. The elements of the Lord's Supper do not changed into Jesus' actual body and blood as the Roman Catholics believe. This view is called Transubstantiation.[152] Neither is Christ present in or around the elements (the "Consubstantiation" view).

---

[152] The Transubstantiation view is based on the *letteral* interpretation of "This is my body" (Matt 26:26), and "this is my blood" (Matt 26:28). This view is rejected, among other things, because the verb "is" (1 Cor. 11:24) can mean "represents" (John 8:12, 10:9, 1 Cor. 10:4).

The Views of the Lord's Supper

	Name	Explanation
The Roman Catholic	Transubstantiation	The elements are changed into the actual body and blood of Jesus.
Martin Luther	Consubstantiation	The elements do not change into the actual body and blood of Jesus; however, Christ is bodily present in the Lord's Supper and His body is received by all who partake of the elements. Christ is corporeally in, under and with the elements.
John Calvin	Spiritual Presence	There is a spiritual presence of Christ at the Lord's Supper.
Ulrich Zwingli	Memorial	The Lord's Supper is a memorial of Christ's death.

    c.   The purpose of the Lord's Supper

        i.   Remembering the Lord: Jesus said we are to remember Him when we partake of the bread and drink of the cup (Luke 22:17-20; 1 Cor. 11:24-25).

        ii. Communion in the body of Christ: Paul used the word *koinonia* in referring to the cup and bread in 1 Corinthians 10:16. Specifically, he was speaking of the communion in the Body of Christ. When we partake of the bread and the cup, we are having fellowship with one another. It is an affirmation that we belong to the same body, have the same Christ and His Spirit, and focus on the same glorious hope.

iii. Eschatological hope: Jesus looked forward to drinking the fruit of the vine "anew" in the Kingdom of God (Mark 14:25; Matt. 26:29; Luke 22:18). Paul saw the Supper as the proclamation of the Lord's death until He returns (1 Cor. 11:26).

There is, therefore, the *upward* (remembering the Lord), *inward* (communion in the Body of Christ) and *forward* (eschatological hope) aspects of the Lord's Supper.

d. The Lord's Supper is administered to believers only (Acts 2:41-42, 20:7; 1 Cor. 10:16).

e. Believers must be in proper relationship with the Lord and with other believers (1 Cor. 11:28).

f. Believer must not participate in the Lord's Supper in an unworthy manner (1 Cor. 11:27-29).

g. Church membership is not a condition for participation in the Lord's Supper. This is the "table of the Lord" (1 Cor. 10:21), not the "church's table." This is evident from the fact that the individual is asked to examine himself and his fitness to come to the Supper. The church is not authorized to sit in judgment upon believers, except in case of disorderly conduct, false teaching or participation in unscriptural practices (1 Cor 11:27-32).

Applications

1. Seek ways to maximize the potential of all believers. Empower and motivate others to be involved in His vineyard. The ministry is not to be done by one person alone.

2. The church is God's people. Spend His resources in building His people, instead of physical buildings. He is more interested in building lives. Our interests must be likewise.

Questions

1. How do you maximize the gifting of church members in your church, especially those of women?

2. What are some of the traditions in your church that are good? Which ones are biblical? Which ones are unbiblical? Which ones need to be changed?

The Doctrine of the Last Things (Eschatology)

Objective

To understand things pertaining to the future, as revealed in the Word, and to live today in light of them.

Introduction

Eschatology is the study of the end times. History has a goal. It has an end. It is not an endless cycle.[153] At the end of

---

[153]The classical Hindu view is expressed by Samartha: "the possibility of values being realized either fully or partially in history is discounted. Since the end of the world eras is *pralaya* which destroys both the good and the bad in history and since the end of the cosmic cycle is only a return to the beginning, there is no room for judgment or the consummation of history.' (Frank Whaling, *An Approach to Dialogue with Hinduism*, p. 69.)

time, Christ shall return, there will be judgment, and consummation of history.

The Return of Christ

The Bible promises Christ will return (Dan. 7:13-14; Mal. 3:1-5; Matt. 24-25, 16:27; Mark 13; Luke 21; Acts 1:11; 1 Cor. 15; 1 Thess. 1:9-10, 2:19, 3:13, 4:13-18, 5:23). This is the glorious hope of the church (Titus 2:13; 1 Pet. 1:3; 2 Pet. 3:9-13; 1 John 3:2-3).

The phases of Christ's return

There are two phases for Christ's second coming. The first phase is His coming to receive His own (1 Thess. 4:13-18; 2 Thess. 2:1; John 14:3; 1 Cor. 15:51-54). The second phase is His coming to earth to establish His millennial rule on earth.

The 1st phase of Christ's return

1. The place: Jesus will come to mid-air (1 Thess. 4:13-18).

2. The procedure: Christ will *return*, followed by the *resurrection* of the dead in Christ, and the *rapture* will occur for believers living at the time of the glorious *reunion*.

   According to 1 Thessalonians 4:13-18:

   a. Christ will return with our departed loved ones.

   b. The dead in Christ will be resurrected (cf. 1 Cor. 15:51-54).[154]

---

[154]This is the resurrection of believers in Christ during the church age. Old Testament and tribulational believers will be resurrected at the end of the tribulation period to reign with Christ (Isa. 26:19; Dan. 12:1-2; John 5:29;

    c.   Christians living at that time will be raptured. There will be a transformation of believers in Christ (1 Cor. 15:51-54).

    d.   There will be a reunion with loved ones. We will meet our loved ones.

3. The purpose of the first phase of Christ's coming:

    a.   To receive His own for marriage with the Lamb of God (Rev. 19:6-8).[155]

    b.   To reward believers for their service to the Lord. Christ will judge believers (not for salvation) and bestow rewards upon them. This is the *bēma* judgment.[156] Believers are to give an account of their service to the Lord (Matt. 25:14-30, 20:1-16; Luke 14:14, 19:11-27; 1 Cor. 3:11-15; 2 Cor. 5:10; Rom. 14:10-12; 1 Thess. 2:19, 4:13-17; 2 Tim. 4:8; 1 John 2:28).

    c.   To remove the restraining power of the Holy Spirit (2 Thess. 2:6-8)[157] so wickedness will be unleashed during the Tribulation.

Rev. 20:4). Unbelievers will be resurrected at the end of the millennium to stand before His judgment seat (Rev 20:11-15).

[155] The aorist tense "has come" in Rev. 19:6 means a completed act. That is, the marriage has taken place before His return to earth. The marriage will take place between the rapture of the church and the second phase of His return.

[156] The bēma judgment is for believers. The Great White throne judgment at Rev. 20:11 is for unbelievers.

[157] There are various views on the identity of the Restrainer. There are a number of factors which provide a positive identification that the Restrainer is the Holy Spirit: (a) Since the Antichrist is a person and his operation involves the spiritual realm, the Restrainer must be a person and a spiritual being; (b) the Restrainer must be stronger than Satan and the Antichrist; (c)

4. The timing: Christians differ on the timing of the first phase of Christ's return and the rapture of the church. Various views are as follows:

   a. Pre-tribulation: The rapture of the church and the first phase of His coming occur before the tribulation period.[158]

Since the theater of sin is the whole world, the Restrainer must not be limited by time or space; (d) the Restrainer will not be a "resident" after the conclusion of the Church age. These four characteristics lead us to identify the Holy Spirit as the Restrainer. That the Holy Spirit restrains sin is seen in both Old and New Testaments (Eph. 4:30; Isa. 59:19; Gen. 6:3). There is a problem with the use of the neuter gender in 2 Thess. 2:6. But Paul uses the neuter gender to refer to the Spirit in Romans 8:16, 26 which would strengthen our view. Another problem raised by some scholars is that they cannot understand how a small army of "half-converted Jews" can get more converts in 7 years without the Holy Spirit than the entire church has been able to win in 20 centuries, with His abiding presence. When we say that the Holy Spirit is not resident, we do not mean that He is inoperative. He is still saving souls but no longer baptizing them into the Body of Christ. Did not a great city repent in sackcloth under the preaching of Jonah? Was not the land swept by a mighty revival under the days of Josiah?

[158]There are many arguments for this position especially from the book of the Thessalonians: (1) The Thessalonians were expecting His imminent return to deliver them from the coming wrath (1 Thess. 1:10). If they were expecting to go through the tribulation, in whole or in part, Paul would have told them to get ready for the painful period. The gospel is only good news in terms of salvation from their sins, but not good news in terms of their deliverance from the Tribulation period. (2) In 1 Thess. 4:13-18 the Thessalonians were sorrowful for their departed loved ones, but Paul comforted them that their departed ones and the living will be reunited at His coming to mid-air. If the living saints were expected to go through the tribulation, they would have rejoiced at their departure to be with the Lord having escaped the Tribulation, and the living would be sorry that they will be facing the painful Tribulation. (3) 1 Thess. 5:9, God "did not appoint us to suffer wrath but to receive salvation through our Lord Jesus Christ." That is good news. (4) In 2 Thess. 1:3-10 Paul comforted the Thessalonian Christians who were going through persecution that they would be given "relief." If they were to go through the Tribulation, Paul would have said to them, "Sorry, brace yourselves for more persecutions during the

```
                    Rapture
     Church age       ↑
     _____
                    ←--7 years --→←-----1000 years →
```

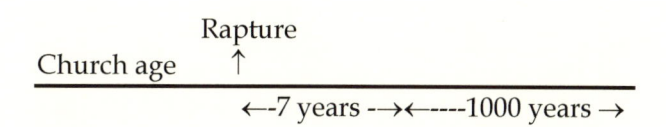

b. **Mid-tribulation:** The rapture of the church and the first phase of Christ's return occur during mid-tribulation. The church will, therefore, go through 3 ½ years of the Tribulation before being raptured.

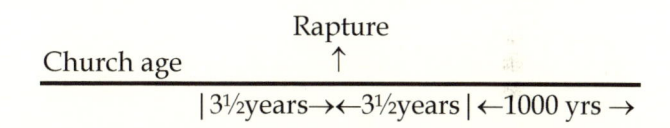

```
                    Rapture
     Church age       ↑
     _____
                    | 3½years→←–3½years | ←1000 yrs →
```

c. **Post-tribulation:** The rapture of the church and the first phase of Christ's return occur after the tribulation period. The church will, therefore, go through the entire 7 years of Tribulation before being raptured. This will be immediately followed by the second phase of His return.

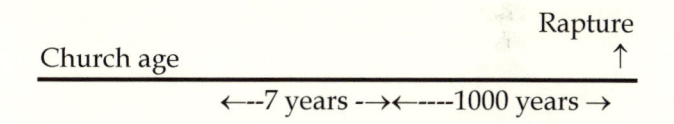

```
                                    Rapture
     Church age                       ↑
     _____
                    ←---7 years --→←-----1000 years →
```

d. **Partial rapture:** Believers who are "watching" and "waiting" for His return will be raptured before, during and after the tribulation period.

Tribulation. No relief yet!" (For a full argument, consult D. Edmond Hiebert, *The Thessalonian Epistles* [Chicago, IL: Moody Press, 1971.])

```
                        Rapture  Rapture    Rapture
   Church age             ↑        ↑          ↑
   ─────────────────────────────────────────────────
                        ←--7 years --→←-----1000 years →
```

The 2nd phase of Christ's return:

1. Christ will descend on Mount Olives (Zech. 14:4) and return to reign on earth (Rev. 20).

2. His return will be:

   a. Personal ("This same Jesus…" Acts 1:11).
   b. From heaven (Acts 1:11; "He is coming with the clouds…" Rev. 1:7; Dan 7:13).
   c. Publicly (Zech. 12:10; Matt. 24:30; Acts 1:11; cf. Rev. 1:7).
   d. Accompanied by angels (Matt. 16:27; Zech. 14:5; Matt. 16:27; Jude 14).
   e. Accompanied by believers (Col. 3:4; Rev. 19:1-9).

3. *The purpose of the second phase of His return:*

   a. To defeat His enemies at the battle of Armageddon (Rev. 19:11-21).

   b. To judge the nations before allowing them into the millennial Kingdom[159] (Joel 3:11-17; Matt. 25:31-46; Acts 17:31; 2 Thess. 1:7-10).

---

[159]This is the judgment of the nations, different from the judgment stated in Rev. 20:11-15. The differences are:

Joel 3:11-17; Matt 25:31-46	Rev 20:11-15
Christ seated on His glorious throne	Christ seated on a great white throne
Took place on earth (Joel 3:17)	Took place in the skies. Earth and sky flee from His presence

c. To bind Satan and his followers for the 1,000-year reign (Rev. 20:1-3).

d. To remove the curse on creation as a result of Adam's Fall and to restore creation to its prosperity and glory (Isa. 2:2, 11:1-9, 35:1-10; Eze. 47:1-12; Zech. 14:4-8, 34:25-26; Rom. 8:19-22; Heb. 9:28).

e. To establish His Kingdom (Rev. 20 cf. Dan. 7:13-14; Rev. 11:15; Isa. 2:2-4, 9:6-7; Zech. 14:16-19; Mic. 4:1-3).

5. Christians are divided over the timing of the second phase of Christ's return. Various views follows:

   a. Pre-millennial: Christ shall return before the millennium.

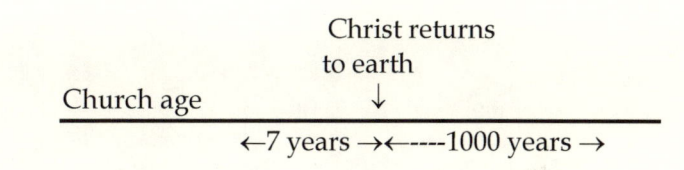

   ```
                          Christ returns
                             to earth
           Church age           ↓
          ─────────────────────────────────────
                        ←7 years →←----1000 years →
   ```

   b. Amillennial: There is no millennium. Both good and evil will continue until the end when Christ returns, and there will be a general resurrection and judgment for all people.

   c. Post-millennial: Christ will return after the millennium. Most post-millennialists define the

Before the millennium	After the millennium
All nations are gathered	Only the dead are gathered

213

tribulation period as now and present, instead of the literal 7-years of Tribulation, and the millennium as the long period of righteousness and peace instead of the literal 1,000-year period. Postmillennialists believe the church will usher in the millennium of Christ through the preaching of the word and the conversion of the world.

```
                                    Christ returns to earth
         Church age                                        ↓
    ─────────────────────────────────────────────────────────
    ←--- tribulation --→←—long period of righteousness & peace→
```

The Tribulation period

The 7-year Tribulation (Dan 9:24-27) is sandwiched between the first and second phases of His coming. The Tribulation period is:

- *"... awful.... None will be like it. It will be a time of trouble for Jacob."* (Jer. 30:7)
- *"...a time of distress such as has not happened from the beginning of nations until then."* (Dan. 12:1)
- Of *"...great distress, unequaled from the beginning of the world until now — and never to be equaled again."* (Matt. 24:21)
- *"that day... will close on you unexpectedly like a trap."* (Luke 21:34)
- *"...the coming wrath."* (1 Thess. 1:10)
- *"...the hour of trial that is going to come upon the whole world to test those who live on the earth."* (Rev. 3:10)
- *"...the time of God's wrath on earth."* (Isa. 24:17-21, 26:20-21, 34:1-3; Rev. 6-19).

The Resurrections

The Bible presents different orders of resurrection:

Name	Time	Event	Judgment throne
First resurrection	At the 1st phase of His return	Resurrection of the dead in Christ (1 Thess. 4:13-18; 1 Cor. 15:23). Rapture of the living saints (1 Thess. 4:13-18)	Bēma judgment (1 Cor. 3:11-15; 2 Cor. 5:10)
	At the 2nd phase of His return	Resurrection of Old Testament and tribulation saints (Dan. 12:1-2; Isa. 26:19; John 5:29; Rev. 20:4-5, 11-13)	
Second resurrection	After the millennium	Resurrection of all unbelieving dead (Rev. 20:5, 11-13)	Great White Throne judgment (Rev. 20:11-13)

Paul says in 1 Corinthians 15:51-54, *"Listen, I tell you a mystery: We will not all sleep, but we will all be changed-- in a flash, in the twinkling of an eye, at the last trumpet. For the trumpet will sound, the dead will be raised imperishable, and we will be changed. For the perishable must clothe itself with the imperishable, and the mortal with immortality. When the perishable has been clothed with the imperishable, and the mortal with immortality, then the saying that is written will come true: "Death has been swallowed up in victory."*

We will be given new bodies. The final redemption is not *escape from* the material, but *invasion of* the earthly and spiritual by the spiritual and eternal. God's goal for His creation is not to *obliterate* it as other religions taught, but to *transform it* and restore it, for originally it was created good; but it has fallen not because it was physical but because it was in rebellion.[160] G. K. Chesterton pointed out that Eastern philosophy inevitably leads to contempt for life, whereas a Judaeo-Christian view leads to contempt for death. In biblical terms it is death that is the enemy, not life; it is existence in a non-corruptible *body* that is our final, hope-for state – not existence without a body.[161]

The Marriage Supper

There will be a marriage supper on earth. The marriage of the Lamb (Rev. 19:6-8) is different from the marriage supper (Rev. 19:9):

The marriage of the Lamb (1Thess. 4:13-18; Rev. 19:6-8)	*The marriage supper (Rev. 19:9)*
Takes place in heaven	Takes place on earth
Takes places before His return to earth	Takes place after His return to earth
The bridegroom is Christ and the bride is the church	The bridegroom and the bride are displayed to both Jews and Gentiles during the millennium
Only for believers during the church age	Those invited to the Lamb's marriage supper include His friends as well as the bride. This implies the presence of other believers besides church saints at this celebration. These would be Tribulation martyrs and believers who will live through the Tribulation and enter the Millennium alive (cf. 12:13-17;

---

[160] John Snyder, *Reincarnation vs. Resurrection,* p. 60.
[161] Ibid.

	20:4-5; Matt. 22:11-14; 25:1-13). They may also include Old Testament saints who will experience resurrection at the beginning of the Millennium (cf. Isa. 26:19; Dan. 12:2).

There will be the wedding of the Lamb of God in heaven between the first and second phases of His return. After His second phase when He returns to earth, there will be the marriage supper (on earth).

The binding of Satan

Satan will be bound for a thousand years. He will be thrown into the Abyss, locked, sealed and kept from deceiving the nations until the thousand years end (Rev. 20:1-3).

The Millennial Kingdom

At His Second Advent, Christ will establish His millennial kingdom. He will rule on earth to fulfill the promise made to David in the Davidic Covenant (2 Sam. 7:12-16). God promised David's descendant (Messiah) would sit on the throne of David forever. Christ did not establish His kingdom on earth during His First Advent, but He will establish His kingdom during His Second Advent. This does not mean kingdom ethics are not applicable to us today. We are to live the kingdom here and now, but there will be a literal kingdom with Christ as the ruling King on earth. At that time, the promises of the Abrahamic and Davidic covenants will be fulfilled (Gen. 15:18-21; 2 Sam. 7:12-16).

During the millennium, Christ will rule (Dan. 7:14; Rev. 19:15) from Jerusalem (Isa. 2:3, 24:23, 33:20-24; Zech. 14:7-10;

Psa. 48). There will be peace (Isa. 2:4, 19:23-25; Zech. 8:4-5), prosperity (Isa. 35:1-7; Amos 9:14; Psa. 72:12-13) and a full knowledge of the Lord (Isa. 2:1-3).

The final rebellion, and the judgment of Satan and his angels

Satan will be set loose for a while after the millennium to deceive the nations (Rev. 20:7-9, cf. Ezek. 38, 39), but he will be defeated. Satan and his angels will be thrown into the lake of fire (Rev. 20:9-15).

The New Heavens and New Earth

At the consummation of all things, God will destroy the elements with intense heat (2 Pet. 3:12). There will be a new Earth that will be home to the righteous (2 Pet. 3:13).
There will be:

- No more evil (Rev. 20:10, 21:27)
- No more sea (Rev. 21:1)
- No more tears (Rev. 21:4)
- No more death (Rev. 21:4)
- No more sorrow (Rev. 21:4)
- No more pain (Rev. 21:4)
- No more night (Rev. 21:25)
- No need for sun and moon (Rev. 21:23)
- No more curses (Rev. 22:3)

There will be:
- A new Jerusalem (Rev. 21:2)
- Gold in the city (Rev. 21:21)
- A river with the water of life flowing from God's throne (Rev. 22:1)
- Twelve crops of fruits (Rev. 22:2)
- The throne of God and the Lamb in the city (Rev. 22:3)
- Access to tree of life (Rev. 22:14)

- Freedom in entering the city (Rev. 22:14)

Above all, God will be with us forever. *"Now the dwelling of God is with men, and he will live with them. They will be his people, and God himself will be with them and be their God."* (Rev. 20:3)

Hallelujah! Praise the Lord! Amen, Amen.

Applications

1. Do not try to predict the date of His return. *No one* knows the time of Christ's return (1 Thess. 5:2; 2 Pet. 3:10). Many people who tried to predict the date of His return, and they have made a fools of themselves!

2. The purpose of the prophecy is not to satisfy the curiosity of our minds, but to challenge us to godly living. The Bible always links the hope of His Second Coming to present-day living (1 Thess. 1:3; Titus 2:13-15; 1 Pet. 1:13, 3:15-16; 1 John 3:2-3). Whatever position you hold about the timing of the rapture or Christ's Second Coming, live today in the light of His imminent return. Prophecy gives rise to piety. We are not to watch the sky; we are to watch how we live.

3. Rather than fearing what is to come, we are to be faithful until Christ returns. Instead of fearing the dark, we're to be lights as we watch and wait. Be faithful until His return.

Additional notes

What Happens to a Person After Death?

Category	At death	Bodily Resurrection	Judgment	Eternal Destination
Christian	Christ's presence	Resurrection at the Rapture	Judgment seat of Christ in heaven	Heaven
OT Believers	Christ's presence	Resurrection at Christ's 2nd coming	Judgment on earth	Heaven
Tribulation Believers	Christ's presence	Resurrection at Christ 2nd coming	Judgment on earth	Heaven
Millennial Believers	Christ's presence	Resurrection at the end of the Millennium	Judgment on earth	Heaven
All Unbelievers	Sheol/Hades	Resurrection at the end of the Millennium	Judgment at the Great White Throne	Lake of Fire

Conclusion

Congratulations! You finished the book! There is so much more to learn, but at least this book gives you a starting point and whets your appetite for more learning, being and doing.

These doctrines are important for building a biblical worldview which will help you discern teachings contrary to God's Word. Be faithful. Be loving until His return. I look forward to seeing you in the New Jerusalem!

God bless you!

Appendix :

The 70 Weeks of Daniel 9:24-27

Introduction

Daniel 9:24-27 is one of the most significant prophecies of the Bible. It is the key to understanding the prophetic outline of history.

Context

Daniel 9 opens with Daniel studying the Holy Scriptures. As he was reading the scroll of Jeremiah, especially chapters 25 and 29, he spent time in the chapters focusing on the prophecy from God about the 70 years involving the captivity in Babylon, and how God would visit the Jews to restore them to the Holy Land. Daniel was taken captive in 605 B.C., and he was reading the scroll in 536 B.C. He concluded that the 70-year captivity was just about to come to its completion and that the time had come for the chosen family to turn their faces homeward.

It was on that occasion when Daniel bowed before God in deepest humility, importuning the remembrance of heaven and the return of the chosen family back home, that God revealed to him the entire future of the world. While Daniel was praying, it was during the time when the lamb would have been sacrificed and offered before God. God gave to Daniel, through the angel Gabriel, a divine revelation from heaven: *The 70 weeks*.

Interpretation of the 70 weeks

Daniel was told there would be a time set for the coming of the King and the millennial reign of the Messiah. There would also be a commencement time and an ending time. Between the two periods, there are 77 years, which equates to 490 years.

The 77s are to be interpreted as 70 times 7 (70x7=490) "years" because 490 days would be meaningless in the context. Moreover, Daniel was thinking in terms of the 70-year captivity. He could have easily moved from the idea of one week of years to 70 weeks of years.

The dealings of God with the Jews during these 490 years could be made to yield six results:

1. to finish transgression,
2. to put an end to sin,
3. to atone for wickedness,
4. to bring in everlasting righteousness,
5. to seal up vision and prophecy, and
6. to anoint the most holy.

The six results may be divided into two classes: the first three are concerned with the removal of sin and the last three with the bringing in of righteousness.

Daniel was to: *"Know and understand this: From the issuing of the decree to restore and rebuild Jerusalem until the Anointed One, the ruler, comes, there will be seven 'sevens' and sixty-two 'sevens.' It will be rebuilt with streets and a trench, but in times of trouble."* (Dan. 9:25)

There has been a difference of opinion as to which decree is referred to here.[162] But only the decree of Artaxerxes

---

[162]There were four decrees relating to the building activities in Jerusalem: (1) The decree of Cyrus in 536 B.C. given to Ezra (Ezra 1) to rebuild the house of God. This decree did not rebuild the defenses of Jerusalem. (2) The decree of Darius in Ezra 6. This is just a reiteration of the decree of Cyrus, and it concerned only the rebuilding of the sanctuary. It was true that some Jews did begin to rebuild Jerusalem's walls after Ezra came to the city, but they did not complete their project. (3) The decree of Artaxerxes Longimanus during his seventh year (Ezra 7). This decree was concerned

Longimanus in his twentieth year (Neh. 2) fits the description. There the King expressly gave to Nehemiah the authority to rebuild the city, the walls, the streets, the ramparts and to make Jerusalem once again an actual, viable city. The decree was issued on March 5, 445 B.C. The walls were completed in 52 days (Neh. 6:15). The first two segments, the 7 sevens (49 years) and the 62 sevens (434 years), ran consecutively with no interval in between. Four hundred eighty-three years after March 5, 445 B.C. was March 30, A.D. 33. (Please refer to chart at the end of this section.)

The 483 years would end during the time of Messiah's first coming on earth. Some time *after* the end of this period, Christ would be *cut off* or put to death. The Messiah "will have nothing" (*After the sixty-two 'sevens,' the Anointed One will be cut off and will have nothing.* [Dan. 9:26]). When Christ was crucified, He was without apparent friends or honor. He was rejected by men, treated as a criminal and even forsaken by the Father.

After the cutting off of the Messiah, the people of a coming prince will destroy the city and sanctuary. It seems most likely that the people are Romans, and the prince who is to come is Titus Vespasinnus.[163] *"The end will come like a flood"* (Dan. 9:26) refers to the extensiveness and severity of the destruction of the city. The same expression is used in Daniel 11:10, 22, 26, 40 and in Isaiah 8:8.

There is no lapse of time between the 7 sevens and the 62 sevens, so the first 483 years ran their course successively, without interruption.

---

with only the resumption of the temple services in Jerusalem. (4) The decree of Artaxerxes Longimanus in his twentieth year (Neh. 2).

[163] John F Walvoord, *Daniel, Key to Prophetic Revelation* (Chicago, IL: The Moody Bible Institute 1971), p. 228.

Now the question we have to answer is, did the 70th sevens (7 years) run its course successively, without interruption, meaning it is now past and its prophecy has already been fulfilled?

The construction mentioned in Daniel 9:24-27 makes it necessary to understand what happened between the 69th and the 70th sevens. After the 69 sevens, it is implicitly stated that the Messiah would be cut off. Then the 70th sevens are set off by themselves, as would be expected, if a parenthesis were implied. If the 70th sevens are to run successively after the 69th sevens, the text would have said the Messiah would be cut off *during* the final sevens.

There is then a great interlude between the 69th sevens and the 70th sevens. That interposition is believed to be the day of grace—the day of the church, the day in which we now live.

The pronoun "he" in Daniel 9:27 introduces a new personality into the story at this point. However, there is no pronoun—only the third masculine singular form of the verb indicating that an antecedent is to be sought, and that of necessity in the preceding context. There is only one antecedent admissible, according to the accepted rule that the last preceding noun that agrees in gender and number agrees with the antecedent. This is unquestionably the "ruler" of Daniel 9:26. He was Titus Vespasinnus, but he is now portrayed as one who will come in the future as a final evil personage, the Antichrist. This Antichrist will make a firm covenant with the people of Israel for one seven (seven years). He will permit them to rebuild the Temple for the purpose of offering sacrifices and oblations to God. They will look upon him as their man of destiny.

But when all appears to be going well, the man of sin will decree that all Jewish worship must cease in the middle of the seven, i.e. 3 ½ years after the commencement of the 70th seven. The middle of the seven commences that period called "the great Tribulation" (Matt. 24:21, 29; Rev. 7:14), the time of distress for Jacob (Jer. 30:7). The last part of Daniel 9:27 seems to describe the desecration of the Temple. This final period of seven years begins with the introduction of a covenant relationship between the future "ruler" and the people of Israel. This covenant is observed for the first 3½ years, then the special liberties and protections granted to Israel will be taken away, and she will be persecuted during a time of great tribulation.

The culmination of the entire prophecy of the 70 sevens is the Second Advent of Jesus Christ, which closes the 70th seventh of Israel, as well as the times of the Gentiles.

The prophecies of the first 69 sevens have been fulfilled, and the clock is ticking toward the 70th sevens. His promises stand sure, and He will bring to close the history of the world to the honor and glory of His Name.

A PANORAMIC VIEW OF THE FUTURE ACCORDING TO DANIEL 9
by Alvin Low

Daniel 9:24: Seventy sevens are decreed for your people and your holy city to (1) finish transgression, (2) to put an end to sin, (3) to atone for wickedness, (4) to bring in everlasting righteousness, (5) to seal up vision and prophecy, (6) to anoint the most holy.

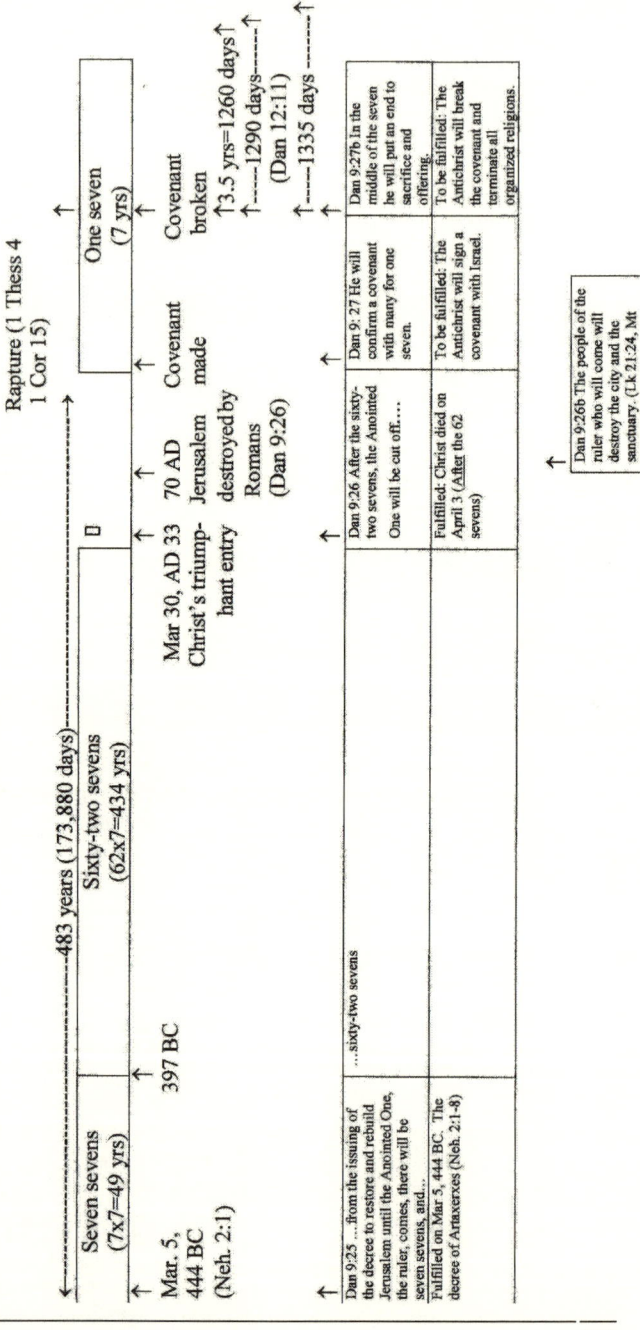

Seven sevens (7x7=49 yrs)	Sixty-two sevens (62x7=434 yrs)		One seven (7 yrs)
Mar. 5, 444 BC (Neh. 2:1)	397 BC	Mar 30, AD 33 Christ's triumphant entry	70 AD Jerusalem destroyed by Romans (Dan 9:26)	Covenant made	Covenant broken

483 years (173,880 days)

Rapture (1 Thess 4, 1 Cor 15)

3.5 yrs = 1260 days
1290 days (Dan 12:11)
1335 days

| Dan 9:25 ...from the issuing of the decree to restore and rebuild Jerusalem until the Anointed One, the ruler, comes, there will be seven sevens, and... | ...sixty-two sevens | | Dan 9:26 After the sixty-two sevens, the Anointed One will be cut off.... | Dan 9: 27 He will confirm a covenant with many for one seven. | Dan 9:27b In the middle of the seven he will put an end to sacrifice and offering. |
| Fulfilled on Mar 5, 444 BC. The decree of Artaxerxes (Neh. 2:1-8) | | | Fulfilled: Christ died on April 3 (After the 62 sevens) | To be fulfilled: The Antichrist will sign a covenant with Israel. | To be fulfilled: The Antichrist will break the covenant and terminate all organized religions. |

Dan 9:26b The people of the ruler who will come will destroy the city and the sanctuary. (Lk 21:24, Mt 23:38, 24:2)
Fulfilled by the Romans under Titus in AD 70.

228

The 483 Years in the Jewish & Gregorian Calendars

Jewish Calendar (360 days per year)	Gregorian Calendar (365 days per year)
(7x7)+(62x7) years= 483 years	444 B.C. to A.D. 33=476 years*
483 years x360 days 173,880 days	476 years x365days 173,740 days + 116 days in leap years** +24 days (Mar 5-Mar 30) 173,880 days

*Since only one year expired between 1 B.C. and A.D. 1, the total is 476, not 477.

** A total of 476 years divided by four (a leap year every four years) gives 119 additional days. But three days must be subtracted from 119 because centennial years are not leap years, though every 400th year is a leap year.

Source: John F. Walvoord & Roy B. Zuck, eds., *The Bible Knowledge Commentary* (Old Testament) (Wheaton, IL: Victor Books, 1985), p. 1363.

Chronological Chart of the End Times

Rev. 21

New Heavens

New Jerusalem

Current heavens & earth destroyed 2 Pet. 3:7, 10, 11

GREAT WHITE THRONE JUDGMENT
Revelation 20:11 - 15

Fire from Heaven destroys rebellion

Satan's Final Rebellion

IT IS DONE
ETERNITY

2nd Resurrection Rev. 20:11

LAKE OF FIRE

Satan Released Rev. 20:7

Marriage of the Lamb
Revelation 19:7-8

HEAVEN

Second Advent: Coming of the Son of man

MILLENNIUM
(1000-Year Reign of Christ on Earth)

BOTTOMLESS PIT

Hades

7 Years TRIBULATION

Satan Bound 1000 Years Rev. 20:2

Judgment Seat of Christ
1 Cor. 3:13 - 15

First Resurrection (Rapture)
1 Thess. 4:15 – 18
Revelation 4:1

Ascension
Acts 1:9

John 19:30

CHURCH AGE

Chart by Dr. Jerry Scolamiero

Unbelieving Israel and Gentiles Judged

230

Bibliography

Ahmad-Shah, E. *Theology – Christian and Hindu*. Lucknow, India: Lucknow Publishing House, 1966.

Benson, Herbert with Marg Stark, *Timeless Healing*. New York, NY: Simon & Schuster, 1996.

Berkhof, Louis. "Attributes of God." *The Living God*. Ed. Millard J. Erickson. Grand Rapids, MI: Baker, 1973.

Daughters, Kenneth Alan. "The Theological Significance of the Ascension." The Emmaus Journal, http://www.emmaus.edu/page.aspx?id=40503.

David, John J. "Unity of the Bible." *Hermeneutics, Inerrancy, and the Bible*. Ed. Earl D. Radmacher and Robert D. Preus. Grand Rapids, MI: Zondervan Publishing House, 1984.

Dickason, C. Fred. *Angels, Elect and Evil*. Chicago, IL: Moody Press, 1975

Fuller Daniel F. "Warfield's View of Faith and History," *Journal of the Evangelical Theological Society* 11 (1968):75-83

Geisler, Norman L. & Ralph MacKenzie, *Roman Catholics and Evangelicals*. Grand Rapids, MI: Baker Books, 1995.

Getz, Gene A. *Sharpening the Focus of the Church*. Chicago, IL: Moody Press, 1974.

Glynn, Patrick. *God – The Evidence. The Reconciliation of Faith and Reason in a Postsecular World*. Roseville, CA: Prima Publishing, 1997.

Hawking, Stephen. *A Brief History of Time: From the Big Bang to Black Holes.* Toronto: Bantam, 1988.

Hiebert, D. Edmond *The Thessalonian Epistles.* Chicago, IL: Moody Press, 1971.

Howard, James Keir. *New Testament Baptism.* London, UK: Pickering and Inglis, 1970.

Lewis, C. S. *A Grief Observed.* New York, NY: HarperCollins Publishers, 1961.

Lightner, Robert P. *Evangelical Theology.* Grand Rapids, MI: Baker Book House, 1986.

Mangalwadi, Vishal. *The Quest for Freedom and Dignity.* Willernie, MN: South Asian Resources, 2001.

Martin, Jobe. *The Evolution of a Creationist.* Rockwall, TX: Biblical Discipleship Publishers, 1994.

Nichols, Bruce J. "Hinduism." *The World's Religions.* Ed. Norman Anderson. London: Inter Varsity, 1950; repr. Grand Rapids: Eerdmans, 1983.

Paché, René. *The Person and Work of the Holy Spirit.* Chicago, IL: Moody Press, 1954.

_____. *The Inspiration and Authority of Scripture.* Chicago, IL: Moody Press, 1969.

George W Peters, *A Biblical Theology of Missions.* Chicago, IL: Moody Press, 1972.

Pillai, Paul. *India's Search for the Unknown Christ.* New Delhi: Indian Inland Mission, 1978.

Pinnock, Clark H. *Biblical Revelation.* Chicago, IL: Moody Press, 1971.

Pudaite, Rochunga. *The Book That Set My People Free.* Wheaton, IL: Tyndale House Publishers, 1982.

Ryrie, Charles. *A Survey of Bible Doctrine.* Chicago, IL: Moody Press, 1972.

_____. *Basic Theology.* Wheaton, IL: Victor Books, 1986.

Saucy, Robert L. *The Church in God's Program.* Chicago, IL: Moody Press, 1977.

Shedd, William G. T. *Dogmatic Theology.* Grand Rapids, MI: Zondervan Publishing House, n.d. 3 vols.

Stephens, Sunil H. "Doing Theology in a Hindu Context," *Journal of Asian Mission* (1/2, 1999):198-99.

Strong, Augustus Hopkins. *Systematic Theology.* Philadelphia, PA: The Judson Press, 1907. 3 vols.

Snyder, John. *Reincarnation vs. Resurrection.* Chicago, IL: Moody Press, 1984.

Tenney, Merrill C. *John: The Gospel of Belief.* Grand Rapid, MI: Wm. B. Eerdmans, 1978.

Thiessen, Henry Clarence. *Lectures in Systematic Theology.* Grand Rapids, MI: Wm. B. Eerdmans, 1979.

Walvoord, John F. *Daniel, Key to Prophetic Revelation,* Chicago, IL: The Moody Bible Institute 1971.

_____. *Jesus Christ Our Lord.* Chicago, IL: Moody Press, 1969

Walvoord, John F. & Roy B. Zuck. *The Bible Knowledge Commentary. Old Testament.* Wheaton, IL: Victor Books, 1985.

Weerasingha, Tissa. *The Cross & the Bo Tree.* Taichung, Taiwan: Asia Theological Association, 1989

Whaling, Frank. *An Approach to Dialogue with Hinduism.* Lucknow, India: Lucknow Publishing House, 2000.

Yao, Santos. "The Table Fellowship of Jesus with the Marginalized: A Radical Inclusiveness." *Journal of Asian Mission* (3/1. 2001): 35-36.

Contact the Author
Dr. Alvin A. Low
2715 Clapton Drive
Colorado Springs, CO 80920
United States of America
www.actsinternational.net
E-Mail: AlvinLow98@yahoo.com